GOOD-BYE
CLUTTER

GOOD-BYE CLUTTER

Organize and Simplify Every Room in Your Home

Susan Wright

Citadel Press
Kensington Publishing Corp.
www.kensingtonbooks.com

CITADEL PRESS books are published by

Kensington Publishing Corp.
850 Third Avenue
New York, NY 10022

First printing 2000

10 9 8 7 6 5 4 3 2 1

Printed in the United States of America

Library of Congress Cataloging-in-Publication Data
Wright, Susan
    Good-bye clutter : organize and simplify every room in your home /
    Susan Wright.
        p.   cm.
        ISBN 0–8065–2134–1 (pbk.)
        1. House cleaning. I. Title.
    TX324.W75   1999
    648'.5—dc21   99—33050
                                                        CIP

Contents

1   The Origins of Clutter   3

2   Clutter Collections   21

3   Uncluttering Your Home   36

4   Managing Your Household Clutterers   55

5   Storage Solutions   67

6   Clothing Clutter   79

7   Home Entertainment   89

8   Paper Clutter   97

9   Clutter-Free Office   111

10   Clutter Sweeps   122

11   Uncluttering Your Time   129

    Index   145

GOOD-BYE CLUTTER

1 : *The Origins of* : *Clutter*

Why does clutter accumulate in your home or office? Where does it all come from? It's not like you make an effort to gather clutter like collectors seek out fine wine or rare stamps. In fact, it may feel like all you do is sort and organize and store things. Then why do you find yourself still inundated with stuff?

Throwing away the things you own involves a risk. Every time you drop something in the trash, you may feel a pang in the pit of your stomach. You may ask yourself "Am I making a mistake?" or "What if I need this later?"

I can promise you one thing: You won't throw away something that is necessary in your life.

You'd be surprised to learn how relatively few things are necessary in your life. And people who have a clutter problem have a long, long way to go before they throw away something that is absolutely essential. What you need to do is to change your attitude about clutter, to not be afraid of the things in your life.

In this book, you will learn a few easy, basic rules for eliminating clutter. By following these rules, you can rest assured you won't be throwing away family heirlooms or putting your bed out for the garbagemen. You will learn to see clutter for what it is—interference. It is the stuff that gets in the way of your more important and valuable possessions.

By applying these basic guidelines to your usual activities, you can tackle your clutter in manageable chunks. No elaborate preparations are needed; no boxes, no string, no endless lists of soul-searching questions. Just guidelines that will help you get the job done.

As you're weeding out the useful things from the useless things that are already in your life, you will find these rules can be turned into handy habits that will become second nature to you and will keep you from accumulating more clutter.

When you have acquired clutter-eliminating habits, then you'll only have to deal with clutter that gathers in your living and work space on a weekly basis. You will only have to give places like closets, drawers, and cabinets a quick once-over once a year.

I call these clutter-eliminating sessions "sweeps" because it sweeps the deadwood from your life. You could do a ten-minute sweep at the end of the week, or an hour-long sweep of your closet every spring. And once you've gotten clutter under control, it won't matter if you skip a week or only do a yearly sweep.

To eliminate clutter from your life, you must face up to why you gather things around you. Even if it's only for a second as you make yourself let go and drop the clutter in the trash. If you're not interested in the psychology of why you collect too many things, that's fine. You can follow the guidelines and never face the source of the problem. But it is easier to form new habits if you understand what it is you're changing and why.

Having a clutter problem is similar to an addiction. Your clutter got this way because you thought you could handle it. And now things are out of control. You will have to make the effort to break old habits and establish new ones. You will have to admit to yourself that your "gut feeling" about things is askew, and unless you learn a better way, you will continue to suffer.

Learning how to let go can be one of the most empowering experiences of your life. And the best place to start is with clutter.

This book is for your if:

- Your home or office is disorganized.
- Your hard drive is full.
- Your closet is filled with clothes you never wear.
- Your medicine cabinet is overflowing onto the sink.
- Your files consist of stacks of paper in drawers.
- Your bookshelves are so crowded you can't find the book you want.
- Your "collections" occupy space on every horizontal surface in your home.

REASONS TO ELIMINATE CLUTTER

You will have room to expand. You can finally but the books or CDs you want, or get all your papers in order in a filing cabinet. You'll have room in the refrigerator for food, and a place where you can find your things when you're rushing out the door to work. You'll also be able to pull a garment from your closet and it won't be wrinkled from being wedged among other clothes.

You will feel good. Clearing the decks is very important psychologically. You'll feel on top of everything, confident, and capable when there's no clutter interfering with your work. You won't be worried about piles with tons of unknown things that need to be done, and that will cut down on your anxiety and depression.

Getting rid of clutter takes less time than dealing with it. When you have to deal with clutter, you have to do it over and over. That is a big waste of time. If you eliminate clutter, you will never have to deal with it again. You'll also get rid of the wasted time of looking through your clutter for the things you need.

You will save money. You may not realize it but you are spending a large portion of your mortgage or rent paying for space to store your clutter. You also pay for moving it from one place to another. Some clutterers also spend too much money on organizers, shelves, containers, boxes, sheds, etc., to hold their clutter.

You will look better. You'll look like you've got everything under control. A clean, efficient work space is impressive to higher-ups and a neat house is a pleasure to invite people into. You'll be able to enjoy the beauty and order in your home and office.

Eliminating clutter is healthier. You'll be able to clean

properly when clutter is gone, eliminating bacteria and dust. Allergies are rampant nowadays, and a clean, uncluttered home can go a long way to relieving symptoms of ill health.

WHY DO YOU HAVE CLUTTER?

I've discovered through my dealings with people who have clutter in their lives that clutter is not just an object, it's a state of mind. There's a lot of fear in a cluttered environment. And often there is shame. Clutter is such an obvious sign that people have lost control of their lives, yet clutter collectors are often highly concerned about maintaining control.

People hang on to something because it is comforting to know it will be there tomorrow. Saving and collecting objects is not bad in itself, but when it serves to bolster your confidence or self-worth, you have a problem. Then you are investing part of yourself in these objects.

When an object carries the weight of a talisman, it takes on a significance that has nothing to do with its inherent worth. This makes you vulnerable. If that object is lost or stolen, it isn't just the crystal vase or the sun hat that gets lost; part of you is missing. If the thought of losing your things terrifies you, you probably have an exaggerated view of their importance. A surprisingly small percentage of your belongings are irreplaceable.

Try this mental exercise. If your house were going to burn down tomorrow, what five things would you want to move safely to a friend's house? Don't include family members or pets, of course. And assume that the insurance company will replace many of your basic possessions—your clothes and furniture, etc. What in your home cannot be replaced?

Usually people want to save photographs, videotapes of important events, personal and professional records, family heirlooms, jewelry, rare books, and fine art. One woman wanted to save all her plants. She had quite a few of them she talked to every day, treating them like pets. One businessman wanted to save his computer because he finally had it modified exactly as he wanted it.

These are the essential things in your life. The other 98 percent of your possessions are replaceable. Rest assured that you could get rid of more than half your things and never even notice it.

Just because something belongs to you doesn't mean you should keep it for the rest of your life. Things are meant to be transitory, but in our culture, somehow they have gained an importance they never deserved.

As you cull the deadwood from your life, you will inevitably get a feeling of confidence. Without needless clutter, your other possessions are easier to organize and are readily available when you need them. Once you've eliminated clutter, you won't have to spend so much time thinking about the things around you. Your possessions will stop getting in your way. And you will no longer have to deal with thoughts of "Ugh! I have to go through those boxes someday," or "I'm so embarrassed for people to see my office this way."

HOW TO ELIMINATE CLUTTER

When you try to hold on to everything, you have control over nothing. Take charge of your life by choosing each object that will stay in your life.

Don't do too much at first. You are attempting to create new habits that will last a lifetime. If you push yourself too hard, you'll fall back into the old habits because it's easier. So start with one room or a corner of that room. It will only take a few minutes a day, and in a week, you will see results.

Don't worry too much about getting started or you'll make elaborate preparations to procrastinate. Instead of tackling the spare junk room or that enormous walk-in closet, you may be more comfortable starting small. Clean one drawer. One shelf. One cabinet. One table. Get rid of one stack of newspapers or magazines. Pack one box.

You don't have to wait until you've got a huge block of time. Eliminating clutter is done one object at a time. Just remember every time you put your hands on something, ask yourself if it's something you use. If you don't use it, you don't really need it. Throw it away.

While some people will want to start with something easy, others may feel compelled to focus on their problem spots: the places that always collect clutter and are always weighing on their minds. They figure once the tough part is done, the rest will be downhill. Either approach works: Start eliminating clutter wherever you feel like it.

The most common excuse for not eliminating clutter is: "I don't have time." But every time you get rid of something, you are saving yourself time. Some efficiency experts estimate that searching for lost things or having to redo work takes up to 20 percent of your time. Eliminating clutter takes no time at all: a few seconds to make the decision, and a couple of seconds to drop it in the trash. Whenever you say, "I don't have time," what you're really saying is, "I don't care." If you care enough, you'll make the time.

Don't waste time sorting and resorting things, lost in indecision. Get rid of things now. The odds are twenty to one that you'll never even remember what you threw away, much less ever need it again.

Step-by-step Clutter Elimination

First, consider each object in your home or office. You are so accustomed to seeing the clutter in your life that you can easily tune it out. You have to pick up each object and hold it in your hand. Think of how and why you got the object. If you can't remember how or why, it's time to throw it away.

Ask yourself: When was the last time I used this object? Or wore this piece of clothing? Or needed this document? If you don't use something at least once a year, it doesn't belong in your life. Throw it out.

Some people have trouble throwing out something even if it's broken because of the meaning invested in it. Make it a solid rule to always throw things away when they break. A broken object is clutter—it's not useful and it's not decorative. The only exception to this is a genuinely valuable antique like a clock or telephone. But if you have a microwave or television you can't use because it's broken, it's clutter. Either get it repaired, or give it to someone who will repair it. And when you get rid of something valuable, try to sell it first. You may find it's not as valuable as you thought.

As you eliminate clutter, you can organize your stuff. The better organized your possessions, the easier they are to find.

The key to organization is simple: Put similar or complementary objects together. Keep the can opener in close proximity to your canned goods. The bathroom cleaner should be in the bathroom. Cookbooks go in the kitchen. And so on.

To do a clutter sweep, start with the top shelf or the bottom drawer or the back of the closet or under the sofa or bed. Go to the most inaccessible spot. Usually the things you don't ever use will accumulate there. Throw these things away.

This downsizing will instantly create space, and you can move useful things into that storage area. Often, useful things accumulate on open surfaces because there's no place to store them—the drawers and shelves are filled with clutter. Make room for the things you use by getting rid of useless "hidden clutter."

In the following chapters, I'll talk more about the techniques of getting rid of clutter as we go through the various rooms in your house, and ways to deal with drawers, closets, and cabinets.

Once you start eliminating clutter, don't reclutter the

area. You can clutter as much as you want to everywhere else, but don't toss those batteries in the drawer you just cleaned out. Find the new place where you decided to store all the batteries and put them there. You may have to resist the impulse to toss the mail on your clean desk; instead, take a moment to open it, throw the junk mail away and file the rest for future action. This is the beginning of creating new habits, an essential part of eliminating clutter from your life.

CLUTTER TRAPS

There are several clutter traps that catch people every time. Stop yourself whenever you use the excuse that you must keep an object because: 1) it's something you might need someday, 2) it's a gift, or 3) it's a treasured memento.

Things You Need

Learn to distinguish between objects you use and objects you need. If you find yourself thinking, "I might need this someday," or "This would come in handy if..." immediately get rid of that object. It is clutter. Most clutter masquerades as something that is potentially useful.

Find something right now that you don't use: an old newspaper clipping, expired coupons, recipes you never look at, much less follow, a dust-covered knickknack. Now throw it away. If you still find yourself holding an object and thinking of a situation in which you might need it, think again. You would need a warehouse to hold everything you "might" need someday. Usually when you finally do need that object, you've forgotten you have it or you can't find it anyway. Throw it away.

Unless you can think of a specific time or place that you will use something, throw it away. You can keep the four half bags of charcoal if you're having a backyard party in a few weeks. But if you don't know the next time you'll ever barbecue, then throw them all away.

Gifts

Gifts can often be clutter wrapped up in pretty packages. Remember the old adage, It's the thought that counts. You aren't betraying someone by throwing their gift away.

If you don't use a gift, and it won't be missed by your mother-in-law or spouse, then give it away or throw it out. The caring and thoughtfulness that prompted the purchase of the gift is the important thing. Why keep that juicer if you don't ever use it? Why keep that bracelet you'll never wear? Don't add to the clutter in your life because you feel obligated.

If you think the gift's disappearance will be noticed, move it from a place of prominence in your living room to your bedroom. From there it can quietly vanish. And things have been known to break. The failure factor will ensure you won't have to live with that enormous barometer for the next ten years just because your grandmother gave it to you.

I've found hidden caches of gifts in people's home they were given or things they bought that they haven't even unpacked from the box. Their excuse for saving these things is, "I may give it to someone." Well, give it away and be done with it. If you don't know anyone at the moment to give it to, then it's clutter. Throw it away.

At some point if a relative or friend is regularly giving you gifts that become clutter in your life, you will have to talk to them. Tell them you don't want to exchange gifts for birthdays, Hanukkah, or Christmas anymore. Tell them not to bring you souvenirs from their vacations. Tell them you are trying to cure an addiction to things and that a clutter expert advised you not to accept any more gifts for at least ten years. It's for your own good.

Mementos

Mementos are another clutter trap. They have all the weight of the past and sentimental associations, and are completely useless. Many people treasure these souvenirs, knickknacks, and tchotchkes. You collect them on vacations and during special events. They seem like they must be important, even if it's only a personalized matchbook or a postcard from Tahiti.

If people give you little knickknacks as gifts, keep them around for a few weeks to enjoy them, then throw them away. These things are meant to be transitory. They were never meant to be kept for years.

Think of a small gift as you would a birthday card—you wouldn't keep a birthday card for years, would you? I hope you wouldn't…if you have, throw them all out right now. The only cards you should keep are those with something personal written in them, not just "Love from Aunt Kate."

People tend to invest the feelings they have on an occasion or for a person into an inherently worthless object. Be confident that you'll remember the important things without the need for a talisman.

Any good-luck piece or ornament is a poor symbol of something that is important to you. Cherish the memory for itself, not for the object you've associated with it. By throwing the object away, you aren't desecrating the memory, you are treating it with the dignity it deserves. The experience of viewing the Grand Canyon is worth far more than the mug you bought at the gift shop.

The same is true for bits of nature that people collect. That pinecone from your ski trip, the rock from the trip to the country, or the shell from that special day at the beach are all clutter. One or two outstanding pieces of nature like a large conch shell or a piece of driftwood can be decorative, but usually the things we pick up are beautiful only in our eyes. Nature is supposed to be transitory, not permanent. Natural clutter tends to disintegrate or collect bugs or gather mold or dust. It's not just rocks and shells—throw out those bouquets of flowers you dried and the ornamental peacock feathers drooping in the floor vase.

If you have trouble throwing something away, you are probably attaching false importance to that object. You own a lot of things, and you've owned many things that are no longer a part of your life. You will own many more things in the coming years. Each individual thing doesn't really matter in the grand scheme of things.

Start seeing your possessions as part of a cycle of objects

that pass into and out of your life. You have to keep that cycle flowing in order to have a healthy, vibrant environment.

ALTERNATIVES TO THROWING AWAY CLUTTER

Some people just can't be ruthless when it comes to their things. Never fear, there are alternatives. You can work your way up to that wonderful light feeling that comes with tossing something in the trash.

Turn unusable objects into something useful. A cookie jar can hold change. Throwaway clothes are cleaning rags. A welcome mat can line the floor of the doghouse. But don't keep an unusable object around because "it may come in handy." If you don't have a job for the object right now, toss it out.

You can also lend your things to a friend. This way you get the best of both worlds—you are getting rid of something, yet you're not losing the object for good. You might even forget your friend has it. Or you'll find you care less and less, because you never really needed it.

If you have a terrible time throwing things away, do it in stages. Fill a box with things you feel you should throw away but just can't make yourself do it. Go through it one more time and throw away as much as you can. Then box up the rest and leave it in a closet. A year later, look at everything again. You'll realize how little you missed these objects, how unimportant they are next to the things you do use. And you may finally feel that sense of well-being you get from living in an uncluttered home. Then you can throw away the box of stuff without another thought.

THE PANG OF LOSS

Inevitably when you eliminate clutter, you will feel the pang of loss. In the beginning, this feeling might be stronger than the object warrants simply because the pain of breaking old habits is not pleasant. It feels wrong because it's not what you're used to doing.

When you remember an object fondly after it's too late to retrieve it, your psychological attachment to clutter will kick in. You'll convince yourself that all those reasons you had before for saving that piece of clutter are still valid. You'll want it back. You may feel awful that you threw away that clock your mother gave you or the worn-out baseball cap you wore for fifteen years. Or the thirteen-year stack of *House & Garden*.

All I can say is ignore those feelings. Or better yet, use them to remind yourself that you have a problem with clutter. No matter how bad you feel now, in a day or a week or a month, you won't care. In fact, throwing something away can imprint it on your mind better than keeping it hanging around. Now you'll never forget how much you care about your mother's thoughtfulness. You'll never forget the shape of the cap you liked so much, which will help you find a new one that's similar. You'll never read a *House & Garden* the same way again.

Rest assured. I've talked to panicked people over the

years who are convinced they have made a terrible mistake by throwing something away. I've felt it myself, and I've always had a pared-down attitude toward life. My family moved quite a bit when I was growing up, and I became used to sorting through my possessions and leaving some behind whenever we made a fresh start. I began to view it as an exciting process, one that prepares you for new adventures.

When I was just out of college, I learned how painful it can be to eliminate clutter, but also how important. I had gotten very attached to a pair of tennis shoes but they had become unwearable, and since I was backpacking through Europe, I didn't want to carry the extra weight. I couldn't bear to throw them out, so I deliberately left them behind in a hostel in Switzerland. By the time I reached France, I was in real pain over the loss. I had bought the shoes in Washington, DC, on a memorable vacation. They fit like a glove from the moment I put them on, and were splattered artistically with paint. People noticed them, and I loved them.

I felt bad about losing those beloved "mementos" for nearly a year. I couldn't believe I had abandoned them under the nightstand at the hostel. But you know what? I got over it. If I hadn't thrown them away then, they would have died in the back of my closet, only noticed and remembered over the next ten or fifteen years when I pulled the out of my way as I searched for something else I needed. Then the shoes would have become a millstone around my neck, something vaguely resented yet necessary to my well-being. Exactly like bronzed baby shoes—something you're "supposed" to keep and treasure, as if bronzing them makes them inherently more valuable.

I'm sure I would have eventually thrown the shoes out, and probably would never have thought of them again. But since I chose to get rid of them so dramatically, they will always be a memory of that treasured trip to DC and my journey through Europe.

No matter what you throw away, family records or heirlooms aside, you won't regret it for very long. In fact, you could suffer a much worse fate by keeping all those things and letting them interfere in your life.

One final word: You don't have to become compulsive about eliminating clutter. The process of developing new habits and creating new attitudes is tough enough without expecting you'll do it perfectly.

The goal is to clear up your life enough so that clutter is no longer a problem. If you're agonizing over the fact that you've cleared out your garage but your backyard still looks like a junk sale—relax. You've accomplished something already. Allow yourself to feel that satisfaction, and then press on. In the end, it will be worth it.

Helpful Hints

- As long as you hold on to valuables, heirlooms, and business and family records, you'll never throw away something that is necessary in your life.

- Put "like" things together.
- Consider each object and ask yourself, "Do I use this? When was the last time?"
- The object is clutter if you say, "I might need this some-day."
- A broken object is clutter—it's not useful and it's not decorative.
- Gifts are often clutter in disguise.
- Don't attach false sentiment to things.
- You'll get over it if you feel bad about throwing some-thing away.

2 : *Clutter Collections*

Some people go out of their way to amass clutter. They call it their "collection." There's an easy way to tell the difference. A collection is meticulously tended, with each item given a place of honor. Clutter is usually a bunch of unrelated objects jumbled together or spread haphazardly around the house, waiting to be sorted and organized.

Is a well-kept stamp or coin collection clutter? No. Take a look at a fine-art collection to see the care with which a true collection must be maintained. So a collection of Beanie Babies or thimbles that have flowed from the end table to the windowsill to the bookcase is not a true collection. It's clutter.

Knickknacks are often referred to as "decoration." You receive them as gifts or buy them yourself when something strikes our fancy: figurines, wall plaques, candles, boxes, etc. Knickknack collecting may be the way you have channeled your collecting instinct, but it can quickly get out of hand.

There are also people who collect information. Are you the type of person who saves magazines and newspapers, moving stacks around and forming ever-increasing piles? Do you clip articles that lie around for months or even years without every being read? Are your bookshelves overflowing with horizontal and vertical stacks? Do you save junk mail to read on a rainy day? That's information collecting gone wild.

Then there are people who collect any object that comes their way: things they find, things their friends are throwing away, even things their spouse tries to get rid of. These people don't necessarily go out and buy more objects, but odd bits and pieces seem to gravitate toward the. Junk is usually saved because people feel like they are getting "a great deal." It costs nothing, and all they have to do is store the stuff until it's needed. That's why junk collecting is insidious. There is a neverending supply of throwaway objects just waiting to be taken in.

If your collecting habit takes up more time than the objects are worth, then you're collecting clutter. If your collection is getting in the way of your day-to-day living, it's clutter. Less is more; overabundance is clutter. Be objective about the items you collect and you will cut down on clutter.

INFORMATION

If you don't have an immediate and clear use for the information, then throw it away. The trick is to sort out the articles or books you think you need from those you use.

Don't keep articles simply because you read them and they are interesting. You'll read many interesting articles during your life. Besides, most magazines are cyclical with their stories. Within a few years, a new article with updated information will be run in your favorite magazine.

If you don't need the information as a reference for a certain project or activity, don't keep the article. You could save an article on hypertension if you're seeing your doctor about yours or a family member's health. You could also save an article on new trends in copy machines if you're going to buy a new copier. On the other hand, you should not save an article "just in case" your copy machine breaks. Remember, most articles are already safely stored in your local library where they are cataloged by subject and author in the periodical section. Often it can be quicker to go to the library and look up exactly what you need, rather than flipping endlessly through a pile of magazines. You can easily find what you need and make a copy.

So only clip an article if it pertains to a project you're working on, or will soon be working on. Then place the article immediately in a specific folder for that project.

If you have file drawers full of project folders, it's time to weed out some "projects." Obviously you'll never have time to do everything. And if you wait years to start, you might as well go to the library to get up-to-date research.

If throwing away all that good information makes you queasy, make a quick note on a sheet of paper of the periodical, title, and the date for each article. A two-inch folder suddenly becomes one sheet of paper in your "future projects" folder. Or keep a notebook that lists the names of articles by subjects. That way, you'll have a neat and handy reference guide for whenever you need to locate an article.

Information on movies you want to see or books you want to buy should go in a temporary "to do" folder. Most people make the mistake of creating new folders for each subject they're interested in. Then the information sits there, never consulted, never acted on.

Your to do folder should be cleaned out every month. If you didn't care enough about the book to buy it that month, you don't need to keep clutter about it lying around.

If you simply can't force yourself to throw away these clippings or magazines, do the same thing as you do for projects—make a list of interesting articles. After a few months, take a look at this list. You'll realize you might not need any of the articles. Then you will feel better about throwing away information in the future.

Whatever you do, don't keep entire newspapers or magazines. I know some people who have collections of *National Geographic,* but those usually fit the criteria of collections: they're organized by date and carefully displayed on a shelf. If your collection of magazines is in piles in your closet, then it's clutter. And it's time to recycle.

People often try to make the exception when their magazines are reference material for their work. Then weeding the clutter from the things you need is a little trickier. Some architects will keep *Architectural Digest,* lawyers will keep the law reviews. But is it necessary? How often do you ever go back to those old trade magazines and look for something? If you haven't used them in the past year, then they are clutter.

Do you have old comic books or other specialty periodicals you've been saving for years, waiting for a time when they will be valuable? Find out if those comics are worth anything, or give them to a local school or your younger relatives. Don't save periodicals unless they are being regularly consulted or used.

If you're an information collector, you're lucky. You don't have to make many decisions during your sorting. Usually, it only improves your quality of life when you dump your piles of periodicals and stacks of clippings. They're a waste of space, they're unsightly, and they're dust collectors. This is a habit that can be cured.

Remember, you can always find any information you need at the library—quicker and easier.

KNICKKNACKS

One way to get over your reluctance to part with your beloved knickknacks is to think of the many things you adored when you were a child. You couldn't imagine living without those toys and games, but you eventually gave them up and moved on. Sometimes children naturally give up toys that no longer suit them, other times an adult helps decide it's time for that moth-eaten teddy bear to go. Even if it was traumatic, remember that your memory of that object is far more important than the object itself. That's because its importance lies in what it means to you.

So you need to get a new attitude about your knick-knacks—an attitude that enables you to let go. Decide for yourself that you will no longer be burdened by an overabundance of *things*. Realize that the quality of your life doesn't rest on having stuff.

Eliminating clutter doesn't mean you can't have nice things in your house. One or two candles aren't clutter, they are decoration. Four or five candles are clutter.

Start slowly. If you can't stand the idea of tossing these precious things in the garage, then wrap them up and store them in a box. You can leave one or two out—your favorites—for display.

After a few months, or even a year, go through the box of treasures. You'll see how little you missed having those knickknacks out and in your way. Oh, you'll think fondly of them when you see them, but notice how often you exclaim, "I remember this one!" You haven't thought about that knickknack while it was packed away because it wasn't necessary in your life.

Deciding which knickknacks to display will be easier because your feelings will be more defined after you haven't seen these objects for a while. Rotate the objects you had out and choose two others to display. Pack away the rest. In a few months or a year, you can go through the process again. You may find that you no longer want to display most of your knickknacks.

Then it will be easier to start throwing away—or giving away the objects you would least like to display.

Don't kid yourself that now that you have all this free space you can buy more knickknacks. If you get something new, put one of the older ones away.

Getting rid of your knickknacks can be difficult at first.

You've invested so much of your care and time on them. You've identified yourself with them for so long. But now you are faced with a unique opportunity to change your life for the better. You can look to the future instead of huddling over your things to reassure yourself of who you are. You can learn to appreciate each object for what it is.

JUNK

Recycling is the wave of the future, and it's good to reuse objects rather than buying new ones. However, most used goods are collected because you think you might be able to use it someday. Beware of this clutter trap. Sometimes junk collectors gather used items because they know someone who can use the object. Usually, they never get around to actually giving the object away again. Or they pick something up because "it's practically new"—that doesn't mean they'll use it.

Only bring home a used object when you know you will use it in the immediate future. If you don't use it in a month or two, throw it out. It didn't cost you anything, anyway. And a great deal isn't a deal if you never needed it in the first place.

I've gone into apartments that only had a narrow passageway through the rooms. The rest of the space was filled with boxes and used pieces of furniture stacked on top of one another. This is the purgatory reserved for junk collectors. And it's a slippery slope. You start out filling one closet, then resort to boxes in one room, which then creep across the floor, expanding right before your eyes. The excuse that it's a perfectly good "whatever" isn't a good enough reason to keep anything.

Odds and Ends

Odds and ends are small junk. They're the little things in junk drawers, on top of your refrigerator, or in the cracks of your sofa. Beware of odds and ends landing on any horizontal surface: mantels, windowsills, ledges, and on top of bookcases, china cabinets, wardrobes, and file cabinets.

Sometimes you put odds and ends in the first open place you find because there is no established place for these things: keys, matches, loose change, etc. Other odds and ends are things that do have a place, but it's easier to toss them in the junk drawer, like tools, string, batteries, empty cassette cases, pens, nail clippers, etc.

These items should have an assigned storage place so you can put them where they belong. Shoe polish, sunglasses, and the lint brush are clothing accessories, and should be stored near your clothes. Coasters and ashtrays should be stored with your placemats and tablecloths, or in a drawer in the living room where they are most used. Safety pins, bandages, hair ties, etc., have their own place in the bathroom or bedroom.

Then there are the odds and ends that you can't identify: a small screw from somewhere, a plastic piece that broke off something, an unidentifiable piece of metal. If you don't know what these things belong to, throw them away. If you haven't figured it out by now, you probably won't ever figure it out.

Matches, candles, and flashlights should be stored together in the same drawer. Of course, it's good to have these things stored upstairs and downstairs, or in the kitchen and bedroom, in case of emergencies. Put a few candles and matches in a handy box in the hall closet or your bedside table. If you need them, you'll be very glad you planned ahead and know exactly where they are.

As for the odds and ends that you don't have a place for, consider keeping them in a drawer that is separated into small sections or containers.

Loose change should be collected in one place. People who have change everywhere are usually the ones who are most dedicated to *not* saving it. They claim it's only temporary, and that's why there are little piles all around the house. Resign yourself to the fact that change tends to collect, and equip yourself with a vase or jar or something that you can use as the central change collector.

Store this change collector in the place where you most often pull loose coins out of your purse or pockets. If it's after grocery shopping, then put a decorative container on the kitchen counter. If your change comes out when you take off your clothes at night, collect it in your bathroom or bedroom. An opaque vase will hide the true nature of the change collector. And by the time you're ready to cash in, it will be worth your while.

Spare keys should always be marked for their use. Don't rely on your memory to know that the pink paperclip means they are the keys to your nieces house. Several years from now, you won't know what they are for.

Your own spare house keys should be marked with what they open and where it is: back door (Oak Street), front door (main office), side door (country house), gate (home), shed (side-yard), etc. Padlocks not in use should always be stored with their key in the lock.

Everyone is afraid to throw out unmarked keys, so don't put yourself in that position. If you have loose keys and you don't know what they are for, keep them in one container together. Over the next year, if you need a key you can't find, go to this spot. After a year or so, throw out the entire bunch and make sure the rest of your keys are marked.

Hanging keys on a key holder is the best way to store them. If you put them in a basket or at the bottom of a drawer, the useless keys mix in with the useful ones. You can have a key holder in your office and one by the door at home or in the utility room. Put the key holder out of the reach of children.

Keys on a ring should have one place where they are stored overnight. Eliminate frantic searches for your keys by placing a hook or a saucer by the front door where you can drop your door and car keys every time you come in. Deliberately make it a habit to not put your keys back in your purse or pocket when you come home. That way, you'll always be able to find them without searching for your coat or purse or looking for wherever you happened to drop them.

PHOTOGRAPHS

Photographs present unique clutter problems. Most of us have our photos in piles and packets and get around to displaying one or two while the rest gather mold in boxes.

Wouldn't you like to have all your photographs arranged for easy display and preservation? No only would you be able to view your photographs, but those messy piles will be gone.

Decide what storage medium you'll be using. Currently the most popular and easy to use are books that hold 4" x 6" photographs. Plastic sleeves hold photographs on each side.

If it's been a while since you looked over your photographs but it seems like you have a lot, buy a few books so you'll have enough to finish the job. To preserve special occasion photos purchase upscale, decorative albums—these can be relatively inexpensive or very costly. Some have a frame and a space in front in which to display one of the photographs.

You can also store and display your photographs on video tapes or CDs. Buy transfer systems for relatively little money, or have it done for you. This is especially good if you happen to have old slides around or if you regularly give slide shows for trainings or as a visual resumé of your work or art.

Digital cameras are best for this because they create a sharp, high-quality image. But you still may want to keep negatives around because the image can't be seen if the tape or disc becomes corrupted.

Sorting Photographs

Gather all the photographs that have been tucked here and there throughout your home. Check boxes, drawers, and file cabinets. I've found photographs on people's shelves and cupboards, on top of the refrigerator, and under the bedroom dresser. Photographs seem to end up everywhere, so check carefully to make sure you find them all.

Don't be dismayed by the pile once you have the photos gathered. The goal is to edit your photo collection into a nice display. In much the same way an editor will cut the film shot by the director, you'll cut some of the photographs. The simple ones to cut are those that didn't come out very well, and the duplicates.

Create a dynamic "show" with your photos so people will flip through them with interest. You might arrange them so that an entire year is captured in one book, or, you can devote a book to your children or grandchildren to chronicle their first few years.

Arrange the photos into a rough chronological order. No matter how you group your photos, they will basically end up in chronological order anyway. Some cameras print the date on the front of photos and some processing houses print it on the back. You're lucky if you've got some dates to go by. Otherwise you'll have to reconstruct the date from the image in the photos.

Make a line of the piles of photos and packets in chronological order along the back of a table, leaving the front half for examining the photographs. Starting with the oldest photographs, go through the first pile. First flip through them slowly to get a feel for what the photographs are about. If you have fourteen of a barbecue and four of your grandkids, you may want to keep three of the grandkids and four of the party.

After you flip through the pile, start pulling out the

photos that struck your eye. These are the ones that look the best. Lay these on the table in rough chronological order. Put the ones you know you don't want in your discard pile.

Now you have good shots, bad shots, and some undecided shots still in your hand. Shuffle quickly through the undecided pile. Put at least half into the "reject" pile, and lay the others out next to the ones you like. Make sure the ones you like the best are closest to you.

Shift these photos into the order they will appear in the book. Remember that after you fill the first slot in the book, the following photographs will fill up a page together. How they look together may determine whether you discard a photo or one to round out a section.

As you sort, you may discover some photos that are out of order. Now the piles can be shifted around or photographs can be moved so all the photos from the beach trip are together, and all the ones sent from your kids at camp are together.

Storing Photographs

Now that you've weeded your photos down, you can begin inserting the photos into the plastic sleeves. As you file your photos, jot down the month and year each photograph was taken. You might do a final edit at this time. Are there photographs that aren't as great as you originally thought, or that ruin the flow of the photos in the book? Now will be the time that this becomes clear.

Don't choose six images of the same scene, like the baby

eating or your husband washing the dog. One or two photos are enough for each special event. And if you keep only the stunning photos, then each one will be savored as you flip through them.

Place the newest discards in a give-away pile to give to your family or friends. It's nice to know that a few of your special photographs will be safe in someone else's home.

Rapidly flip through the discard pile to be sure there are no gems you missed. Then throw out the photos that you don't want and that you aren't giving away. Consider keeping your negatives so that if you absolutely need to, you can make new copies of the photos. File them in a folder called "Photographs" in your file cabinet—and be sure to divide these by year.

Displaying Photographs

Some people crowd the top of their dresser or desk with photographs. This is another case of when too much of a good thing equals clutter. Once you have too many photographs to see each one clearly, it's time to rotate or hang them.

Photographs look much nicer displayed on a wall than crowded behind one another on a flat surface. Consider creating a wall of photos. Rotate photographs in the same way you rotate decorative objects in your rooms.

Only display the most special photographs. Make sure the frame properly complements the image and take time to hang them for a pleasing effect. Photographs are precious and should be treated that way.

If you have many photographs you want to display, then buy the large multi-pocketed frame that holds eight or twelve or twenty photos, creating a collage. Change the photos once a year for variety.

Helpful Hints

- A collection is organized and self-contained; clutter is usually jumbled together or spread haphazardly around the house.
- Throw away information that you have no immediate use for.
- You can always find any reference material you need at the library quicker and easier than sorting through piles or boxes of magazines.
- Two knickknacks are decoration; five knickknacks are clutter.
- Only take a used object when you know you will need it in the immediate future.
- Rather than stashing odds and ends in the first open place, make a place where these things belong.
- Store loose change in one place.
- Spare keys should always be marked for their use.
- Edit your photographs to create a dynamic "show" so people will flip through them with interest.
- One or two photos of each special event is enough.
- Rotate photographs in the same way you rotate the decorative objects in your home.

3 : *Uncluttering Your Home*

An efficient, well-kept household is not an impossible dream. Only two things need to be kept in mind: Get rid of things you don't use and put the things you do use in the area they are used or nearby. This chapter will go through each room in your house and provide solutions to common clutter problems. Storage spaces will be dealt with in a later chapter.

Keep in mind the standard guidelines to clutter elimination. First, start small. Choose one corner or one piece of furniture.

Ask yourself these basic questions as you pick up each object—Do I use this object? Where do I use it? If it is not being used, throw it away. Some professional organizers suggest you can store an object for a temporary time period before deciding to let go. However, storing too many things will defeat your aim of eliminating clutter. By making the choice to throw things away you don't need, you are taking control of your surroundings. Storing something should only be done when you simply can't make yourself throw it away right now.

Consider furniture as well as objects. You don't need things like tiny tables that display clutter, or shelves that organize clutter, or racks that store clutter. Get rid of a chair or two if you only have a few people in your home at one time.

For furniture and objects that have a specific daily function, consider where you use these. If you wear a certain pair of shoes and gloves when gardening, keep them in a cabinet or on a shelf near the door to the garden. Except for rare occasions, activities should be confined to one area of the house. For example, your exercise equipment shouldn't be divided between the living room and the bedroom. If you like to watch television while you exercise, put the equipment near the television. By separating your activities, it will be easier to organize your possessions.

Whenever possible, gather similar objects together and store them in the same room, in the same drawer, or on a shelf. Keep all the games together near the table where you play. If you like to play solitaire before you go to sleep, keep a pack of cards in the bedroom.

You should also have a place to gather things that you need to bring to the office or to your grandmother's house or to the beach on Saturday. Designate a shelf or table and put things there as you remember you'll need them. This will save you from having to remember everything at once when you're on your way out the door.

Don't give in to the urge to fill empty niches with miscellaneous objects. That translates into clutter. Just because an object will fit someplace doesn't mean that is where it should be.

Your overall goal when eliminating clutter from a room is to create open space, a buffer between objects. I've met people who feel compelled to fill every crack and cranny with *something*. They get satisfaction from finding an object that fits into a space. If you feel you are being efficient by doing this, you are sadly mistaken.

Consider the ancient practice of *feng shui*, which deals with the placement of objects to create a balanced environment. One of the first steps is to remove clutter in order to free the energy flowing through a space. Clutter is transitory and insignificant—yet it can infect an entire room with a feeling of chaos and anxiety.

FOYER

The foyer is a general-use area and therefore should be kept clear of clutter, yet it's often the most cluttered room in the home. It's also the first thing people see when they come into your house. Put your best foot forward, so to speak. Don't get in the habit of leaving *anything* in the foyer unless it's on its way out the door imminently.

If objects must be kept in the foyer, be sure to have proper storage for them. The shelf in the foyer's closet should hold things you use often, rather than serving as long-term storage. Coats, sweaters, rain gear, outdoor toys and games, binoculars, and sporting equipment can be kept in this closet.

Install hooks on the inside of the door for outdoor clothing. Hooks are much easier and quicker to use than hangers. Hats, scarves, and gloves tied together with string can also be hung from these hooks. Boots should be stored on a dripping rack on the bottom of the closet nearest the door. A coatrack is good for older children and adults if there is no closet in the foyer. An ornamental coatrack makes for an elegant spot on which to hang guests' out-door clothes. Make sure the stand is put on a waterproof surface to avoid damage by dripping rain or snow.

An umbrella stand is also handy. You will always have umbrellas, and this is the most convenient way to store them. Buy a conventional stand, or a wide-mouthed, heavy vase will also do.

LIVING ROOM

Your general living area has a tendency to get cluttered just through day-to-day activity. Someone brings in the paper, books get left on the floor, glassware collects. The real problem occurs when you have lots of other objects already cluttering your living room. Then it becomes diffi-cult to see the stuff you don't use.

First, clear out the information clutter, the knickknack clutter, and the junk from your living room, following the guidelines in chapter 2.

Then, gather similar objects and store them in the same place. Often a multipurpose wall unit with cabinets and shelves provides the best organizer for your living room. Or, use a sideboard with divided drawers and shelves.

You could keep your heating pad in the side table if you use the pad while sitting on the sofa. With the heating pad could be books to read, reading glasses, a foot massager, your needlepoint bag, etc. Coasters, ashtrays, and matches should be together. As should TV trays, folding chairs, and a card table, and liquor, glasses, ice bucket, tongs, and corkscrew.

Duplicates are clutter. You don't need two ice buckets or three card tables. Unless you use these multiple items (like having more than one ice bucket for large parties), get rid of all but one.

Consider whether every activity that goes on in your living room should continue to be done there. Perhaps it would be better if your sewing kit is kept in the bedroom or the workroom.

If the living room is noisy, keep the phone in the hall, foyer, or kitchen. With the phone should be the white and yellow pages, city maps for locating addresses, pens, pads of paper, and some type of message board. Some people keep their take-out menus near the telephone, too.

If your house has both a den and a living room, designate specific activities for each. You could keep one room neat for entertaining, and allow the other to have a more casual atmosphere where snacks and games are permitted.

When children play in the living room, designate an area that belongs to them. That's where their toy box and furniture should be. If you don't confine children's activities to one area, their clutter will spread out across your entire living room. Make sure there is enough storage space for toys, games, and creative supplies in this area. Impress upon children that this is *their* space and that their things belong in this area, not scattered throughout the house. You can expect maximum clutter when your children mainly play in the living room, while their toys and games are stored in their bedrooms.

BEDROOM

Often bedrooms get cluttered because they are the most private rooms in your home. And you can close the door when visitors come over and they'll never see the mess. This section will deal with the room itself, while closet and storage space will be discussed in chapter five.

The bedside table can hold anything you need while you're in bed: reading glasses, books, flashlight, pen and paper, etc. The surface should hold what you frequently use: clock, lamp, and telephone. Things that you use sporadically like health or beauty aids shouldn't be kept on top of the bedside table—these belong in the bathroom or in a drawer.

If you have space for a desk in your bedroom, place all the things associated with your "home office" nearby: trash can, telephone, lamp, bookcase for reference books, file cabinet, etc. If you have space for exercise equipment, define one area of the bedroom for it.

The top of your dresser should become a catchall for anything and everything. If you need to put your keys and jewelry somewhere, get a box or tray to contain them. Resist the urge to put folded, clean clothes on top of the dresser or the bedside table. It takes no more effort to put them in drawers.

What about the space under the bed? If you can see it, don't put anything there. It's the same philosophy of not filling every crack and cranny with stuff. When you leave space for your eyes to rest in, that creates a spacious flow to your room. If you have concealed storage space under your bed, however, then it's a fairly accessible spot. Store things like luggage, holiday decorations, or boxes of off-season clothing (more on that in chapter 5) there. If you have drawers under your bed, you can store clothes, games, and supplies for projects.

As for the bed itself—making your bed is an easy way to be sure your bedroom looks neat. You should make it as soon as you get up, even if it's only a matter of flipping the covers up and straightening them. You can always deal with arranging the sheets and pillows at night when you're about to use the bed. If two people share a bed, then the last one out of bed has to make it.

Linen

For some reason, linen seems to collect even though much of it is old, worn-out, or no longer useful. You can use these things as rags, but they need to be stored someplace else, not with your useful linen. Get rid of anything that is frayed or worn, and throw away burned pot holders or kitchen towels.

Don't keep rugs or curtains that don't suit your decor. And don't feel you have to keep towels or sheets that were given to you as gifts if they don't suit your sense of style.

KITCHEN

Look at your kitchen counters. Ten to one, you'll find all sorts of things on them that you don't use daily: canister sets, bread box, cookie jar, towel holder, take-out menus, old vitamin jars, knife block, mug stands, decorative plaques, plants, and more, including appliances like a Crock-Pot, toaster oven, toaster, coffeemaker, pasta maker, and food processor, among others. Scale down this clutter by throwing away anything you really never use.

Store everything you only use once in a while in the most convenient place, depending on how often you use them. For example, you can keep your glasses in the cupboard by the refrigerator, but put the coffee mugs on the shelf over the coffee machine.

Before you start moving things around, take mental notes as you work in your kitchen about which things you reach for most often. Could these things be moved closer to the work surface where you use them? If there is something else there, move it up one shelf or down one drawer. Rarely used items should be gathered into one lower drawer.

Your everyday dishes should be easily accessible on a low shelf in your overhead cabinets. Same goes for your drinking glasses. Your top cabinets are for mixing bowls, casserole dishes, baking tins, and stuff of that ilk. Heavier items belong in the lower cabinets: sauce pans, frying pans, roasting pans, broiler pans, pressure cookers.

Baking utensils, including rolling pin, mixing bowls, sifter, baking sheets, and baking tins, can all go on one shelf. If your specialty is candy making or cake decorating, keep those supplies together on one shelf rather than spreading them among drawers and shelves.

Duplicates

Go through each drawer and shelf. If you have duplicates of any of your kitchen items, consider how often you use both at once. If you can't think of a time, get rid of one. If you're keeping a "spare" in case of emergency, don't bother. That sort of thinking would necessitate you owning another house to hold all your spares. Only when something breaks, should you buy a replacement.

Some people believe you can never have too many glasses. They have shelves full of sets and individual glasses. But how many glasses do you really use? If you've got glasses that you haven't used in more than a year, throw them out. Don't use the excuse that you're "saving" glassware or dishware for a "special" occasion. Either have that special occasion once or twice a year or start using those glasses for everyday occasions. Use them or get rid of them.

The same goes for mugs. Some people collect mugs from wherever they travel. This is once again a case of too much of a good thing. If there are mugs in your cupboards that you never use, throw them out. If they mean too much to you, start using them and then get rid of the mugs you like the least.

Appliances and Accessories

Along the same lines, if you don't use an appliance, throw it away. Don't keep that waffle iron just because it might be fun to make waffles someday. If you haven't done it by now, you probably never will. And don't keep appliances that you used to rely on—like your Chinese wok—when you never cook with it anymore. Keep only the appliances you use at some point every year.

If you use canisters, keep them all in one area. If you don't use them but you have them anyway, they are clutter. Get rid of them.

What about that bulky knife block? You can either store your knives in a drawer organizer or in a handy knife holder which folds out of sight and keeps your knives from being jumbled together in a drawer and attaches to the bottom of a cabinet.

A lazy Susan can revive a useless deep corner cabinet. Put your spices, canisters, baking supplies, tea, coffee, canned and dry goods on it. You can also buy lazy Susans with several tiers.

Increase the efficiency of your cabinets by buying racks to display cans and boxes. Or, install narrow wire shelves on the insides of cabinet doors to store condiments or sponges. Put vases, pitchers, and utensil jugs holding wooden spoons, and large utensils in a tall cabinet.

Only leave appliances on your countertop that you use frequently. If you only use your mixing bowl once a month, find a place for it in your cabinets. The same goes for the coffee machine, toaster, juicer, toaster oven, or coffee grinder.

Spice racks are good; they limit the amount of space your spices can take up, thereby ensuring you will monitor which ones are used and which ones are not. Alphabetize your spices. This will take a few minutes at most, and the result will be an organized rack with each spice easily accessible.

Food

Your cabinets and refrigerator are often clutter collectors. But they are also easy to clean. Start at the most inaccessible shelf and work your way down or up. You'll find things you never knew you had, most of which should probably be thrown away. This will free up space for you to better store your food.

Store frequently served items on the most accessible shelf: water, milk, soda, and juice on the top shelf in the refrigerator, and your breakfast cereal and snacks on the bottom shelf of an upper cabinet. A basket is good for holding fruit. It makes a colorful display and puts the fruit where everyone will be compelled to eat it. It also helps keep your fruits fresher longer.

Also group similar foods together.

In the refrigerator, choose a prominent place for leftovers so that you can see them and remember to eat them before they spoil. Don't wedge leftovers into any available space, because those containers will get pushed toward the back and you'll probably never see them again until they emerge, covered with green fuzz.

If you have too many leftovers to fit in your leftover spot, then throw out the oldest of the bunch. It's always a good idea to throw out a leftover when you put a new one in the fridge. Then you aren't fooling yourself and can begin to objectively assess if you need to keep the ones that are already there. The rule is that leftovers shouldn't be eaten after three or four days anyway.

The freezer usually has more wrapped packages of old

food than the fridge. There's a misconception that since it's cold in there, things can be stored indefinitely, but nothing should be stored for more than six months. When you put something in the freezer, be sure to carefully mark the container with the contents and date. When you put a new item in your freezer, put it behind existing contents so you'll use those first and avoid waste. If you haven't instituted this system already, evaluate the contents of your freezer now and get rid of anything you're not sure of.

I once met a woman who could pull Tupperware of every shape and size from her cupboards, and she had duplicates of many. They were stacked according to size and filled up an entire cabinet. When I asked how often she used these containers, she admitted she only used them for leftovers, and that she only really used the larger ones kept on the middle shelf.

We went through her food storage cabinets and transferred half-used boxes and bags of food into various containers. At the end of an hour, she had stackable Tupperware neatly holding food items in her cabinets, and only one shelf of Tupperware waiting for leftovers.

BATHROOM

The bathroom collects clutter quicker than any room in the house. Perhaps it's because bathrooms have limited storage space, or because there are so many health and beauty products available that people think they must have.

Eliminate everything you aren't currently using from your bathroom. Health and beauty aids are not meant to last forever, and should be purchased and used immediately. Be ruthless. These aren't possessions, they're packaged goods that can be bought virtually anywhere at any time.

Manufactured organizers work great in bathrooms—in the shower, under the sink, above the toilet, or anywhere you have available space. Put a large lazy Susan in that deep cabinet under the sink so you can turn it and bring everything in the cabinet immediately to hand. Toilet paper, feminine-hygiene products, and paper cups (if used regularly) should be kept under the sink, if your sink has an enclosed vanity. If you don't have an enclosed vanity, for instance, if you have a pedestal sink in your bathroom, consider skirting the vanity and storing these items on shelves behind the skirt. Bathroom cleaning products can also be kept there.

Things you use in the shower should stay in the shower on a dedicated caddy: shampoo, conditioner, razor, shaving cream, sponge, soap, or what have you. You can get a caddy that hooks over the showerhead, or one that hangs from suction cups on the shower wall.

To organize the storage in your bathroom, first assess the number of shelves and cabinets you have. Then, according to the number of people who will be using the bathroom, designate areas for each person's private storage. Also designate areas for general storage.

One woman I worked with tried to claim two-thirds of the medicine cabinet because she said, "I have more things to put in there than my husband." As trivial as this sounds, her husband was irritated that he was forced to squeeze his stuff into a third of a cabinet to make room for her overflow. I suggested that she throw out some old and unused items and keep her stuff in her half of the cabinet. Not dividing space equally will only cause resentment.

Bathroom storage should follow the usual rule: Put the most accessible things on the most handy shelves. And keep like things grouped together. First-aid items, such as Band-Aids, aspirin, and antiseptic should go next to one another on a shelf or in a box clearly marked "First Aid" kept in the general storage area. Extra towels and washcloths should be stored together in a cabinet, either in the bathroom or a nearby linen closet. Grooming items, such as deodorant, lotion, and tweezers, should be grouped together in each person's private storage area.

If you have a large quantity of makeup, sort it into baskets or boxes and keep it in your private storage. If you have one large makeup box, find an appropriate place for it under the sink or in a large cabinet. Makeup clutter can be a real problem, so get rid of any makeup you aren't using. After a year, throw away any eye makeup, like mascara and eyeliner. Using old makeup can cause an infection. Likewise, foundation can also separate and get muddy looking and cause your skin to break out, so throw it away if it's more than a year old.

Medicine Cabinet

How many bottles of old pills do you have in your medicine cabinet? How many packages of cold tablets with only three or four pills left in the foil-backed holders?

Most people collect medicine without thinking about

it—but this can be dangerous. Expiration dates pass, labels wear or crumble off, and assorted pills with no markings lurk in every corner of your medicine cabinet. The least dangerous thing that can happen is a medicine loses its effectiveness, but that's little comfort when you have a cut or cold. On the really bad side, you might mix up pills, and take medicine for constipation instead of one for a headache. The worst thing that can happen is that you can ingest a medicine intended for external use only because you can no longer read the label.

Any occasionally used external medication more than a few years old should be tossed. Age and air can affect medicine, lessening its effectiveness. Old prescription medication should be thrown away once you have recovered from an illness. Antibiotics lose their effectiveness with time, and there is the risk that your doctor will be unable to properly analyze your symptoms if you've already begun self-treatment with leftover medicine. You shouldn't have any antibiotics left over anyway as you should technically finish your prescription; however, if you do have any left over, get rid of it.

Over-the-counter medicines should be thrown out once the expiration date has passed. If you can't find the date or can't decipher it or don't specifically remember when you bought it (but you know it was more than a year ago), throw it out. Also dispose of pills, capsules, and tablets that you're not sure of. You might want to keep a record of prescriptions you've been given, when you took them, and how you reacted to them—if at all—to give your medical history to a new doctor.

Step-by-step Uncluttering

Don't pull everything out of your bathroom cabinets at once. There is probably some sort of order already imposed on your supplies. You'll need to see what you've got and how it fits on the shelves in order to create a new order out of the current mess.

When you start, remove small groups and make piles of objects on the counter. Try to immediately group likes together. Begin at the top, furthest back corner of the cabinet. There you'll find things that you've forgotten about and never use. Most you can throw away, like the dried tube of face mask and sample bottles of lotion. Anything dusty is probably not worth saving.

Throw out beauty products that you don't use. Why keep products that don't thrill you? You'll never use them again. Also throw out old fragrance bottles, aftershave, cologne, and perfume. These fragrances go rancid after a year on the shelf. Even if only a little has been used, it's better to throw it out than risk smelling strange. Your nose becomes used to a fragrance after constant use, so you may not be aware of odors that others can detect.

Some supplies belong on the upper shelves because accidents do happen. If you can envision a need for them, it would be much more convenient to have the item on hand even if you haven't used it in a year—Ace bandage, tape, gauze, pregnancy test, sunburn relief ointment.

If you find something that you needed at one time but couldn't find, move it to a more prominent position in your cabinet. Tubes of salve, cough drops, or throat lozenges should be grouped visibly together on an upper shelf. They aren't used often, but should be available when you need them.

WORKROOM

The workroom is the best place to assign multiple activities. You can use it as a home office, workshop, sewing room, hobby room, or what have you. The key to keeping a workroom functional is having enough storage for your tools and supplies.

You'll need suitable work surfaces. If a project is not ongoing, remove it from the work surface to make space for other projects. Projects like building models, piecing together jigsaw puzzles, or sewing a dress can take a week or two. Once they are completed, they should be cleared away and the work space left open for the next project.

Proper storage for tools and supplies should be near the work surface, either in a drawer or on a shelf. A row of shelves above the work surface, or floor-to-ceiling shelves nearby, serve as excellent active storage space. Buy plastic bins or baskets to hold your projects together, and to keep one project's supplies from mixing with another's.

General items used frequently—scissors, pens, pencils, rulers—can be kept in an easy-access container on your main work surface.

A Peg-Board over the main work area is a good place to hang larger tools. Here, they'll be visible and within easy reach. Don't be too quick to assign a place to each tool. As you use the board, you may find that certain tools need to be more accessible, and you may acquire tools that necessitate moving the Peg-Board hooks. Place the ones you use most often right above the work surface. Also with this method, you'll be able to easily see which tools you don't use and which you have duplicates of.

The workbench and toolbox need to be cleaned out as well. Do you really need eight jars of screws? Or a box of assorted caulk, glue guns, and cans of WD-40? Do you have balls of twine, batteries, electrical gear, and other stuff invading your toolbox?

Separate your tools from your supplies. Throw away duplicates or worn-out tools as well as old supplies. Get rid of ruined tools like used paintbrushes, rusted pliers, broken shears. Gather the tools you do use along with extension cords, clamps, measuring tape, string, and supplies and separate them neatly into drawers or in a separate toolbox.

Last, don't leave your ironing board up. If that's a habit you can't break, invest in an ironing board that attaches to the back of a door. These are easy to install and you will always have to flip the board back up when you're done so you can close the door. No more problem!

Helpful Hints

- Your overall goal when eliminating clutter from a room is to create some open space, a buffer between objects.
- If you have duplicates, then that's clutter.
- Don't leave anything in the foyer unless it's on its way out the door the next time someone goes outside.

- In the kitchen, store things in the most convenient place depending on where and how often you use them.
- When you start organizing, begin at the top, furthest corner of the cabinet where there are things you never use.
- Health and beauty aids should be thrown out if they aren't being used.
- Don't take everything out of your cabinets at once. There is probably some sort of order already imposed on your shelves that you can work with to better organize your things.
- The key to keeping a workroom functional is having enough storage for supplies and tools.

4 : *Managing Your Household Clutterers*

Clutter doesn't magically appear out of thin air. People produce clutter. So when you want to eliminate it, you have to see that each person in your household assumes responsibility in maintaining order. This chapter focuses on the members of your household and provides helpful hints on how to get everyone involved in eliminating clutter from your lives.

If clutter is a household problem, call a meeting. You can't just grab people as they run through the house on their way to the office or to school. You have to make a strong point to impress upon everyone that things are going to have to change.

Everyone living in your home, whether a roommate, spouse, child, or relative, must acknowledge that clutter is a problem. If you have trouble getting someone to pay attention and take this problem seriously, insist that everyone admit out loud your household has a clutter problem. Then, each person will have to acknowledge out loud that they will take responsibility for making a change.

If everyone makes even a small effort, you can say good-bye to clutter in your house. The community effort will enable you all to pinpoint the problem areas where things tend to gather.

Tell everyone that their uncluttering should not depend on whether the others do or don't adhere to their commitment. Also, different people see different clutter than others. While some may pick up glasses and return them to the kitchen, others may weed through a stack of magazines.

Ask your housemates to commit themselves to leaving a room in better shape than they found it. Read them the following and have them agree to these points:

1. Take anything you bring into a room back out of the room when you leave it.
2. Wipe up spills as they happen and remove leftover food when you go.
3. Rinse off the dishes immediately when you're done and put them in the dishwasher or washing tub or sink.
4. Vacuum or sweep if you make a mess on the floor.
5. Clean off the counter in the kitchen or bathroom after using it.

SPOUSE

When one or both partners are clutterers, you must agree to compromise. Usually each person has his or her own special problem—for example, the husband may be a magazine and newspaper junkie, while the wife has a drugstore in the bathroom.

You have to start out acknowledging each person's right to live as they want to, but that doesn't mean you have the right to inconvenience your spouse. These two principles must be kept in balance, and that requires equality. One person's habits or preferences should not be allowed to disrupt the rest of the household.

Each person needs his or her own private space, including work space, closet space, and storage space. You each should have a work surface, be it a desk or a table with storage nearby. These spaces have to be equal or tensions will rise. Don't make a habit of doing your work in your spouse's work space.

Work or hobbies need to be done in these workspaces rather than in general areas. No one should be allowed to consistently clutter the dining-room table as well as his or her own work space.

Depending on the size of your house, each spouse may have more than one private area. You may each have an entire room for a home office, workroom, or workshop. Determine which areas belong to whom—you may be surprised to discover that one spouse has two rooms of private space (a workshop and a home office) while the other spouse only has a desk in the living room. To promote equality in the relationship, this should be changed immediately.

Even if you don't know what you want to do with your private space, it belongs to you. Turn it into a den where you can retreat. You might be surprised how many marital fights are really "turf wars" caused by your natural instinct to have your own space.

The rest of the house can be designated general-use

space. These areas should be cleared of clutter once a day, unlike your private space, which may be left semi-cluttered if you are in the middle of a project. Set a good example. With private areas designated, it will become increasingly clear who is the cluttered and who is not.

If your spouse claims ignorance as justification for clutter—he or she doesn't know what to do with clothes, paperwork, dishes, or tools—then show him or her exactly where the objects go. The house and your possessions belong to both of you, and you both should know how to take care of them.

Try not to get angry if you live with someone who can't seem to remember or follow through on commitments to keep the house clutter-free. Clutterers don't do it to deliberately hurt you, but often spouses of clutterers take it personally. "He knows how much it upsets me," or "I've told her a thousand times and she does it again and again."

In these cases, it's better to focus on your feelings of oppression and anxiety about the clutter rather than to try to tell your spouse how mad you are. Try to explain how unhappy it makes you feel to live in such an environment. Then ask your spouse why he or she forgot to put his or her clothes in the hamper. If you ask, your spouse will start thinking about it, which is the first step in doing something about it. If you start a fight over it, your spouse will justify not wanting to clean up as he or she fights back.

Usually the only thing that gets people to pay attention to their own slovenly habits is to make them suffer for it. Don't clean the dishes or the kitchen for them. Don't pick up their clothes. Don't pick up the strewn newspaper on

Sundays. Let them live with their mess for a while, and it will begin inconveniencing them. Then they'll have to start thinking about what they're doing.

As a last resort, when things have built up beyond repair, announce that starting next week, on Saturdays, you're going to throw away anything left in the common areas. Then do it. It may cause some anger, but your spouse has not right to clutter both his or her space and yours. As long as you give fair warning, you can explain that you've lived too long in their mess to be able to stand it any longer. Once a week is not too much to ask from anyone to pick up their things.

The first time you do this, sweep everything into a garbage bag. After your spouse has freaked out about what's missing, show him or her the bag full of stuff with a couple of their prized possessions packed away along with a lot of useless clutter. Tell your spouse that out of the goodness of your heart, you'll make this a warning. If it happens again, he or she will be digging through the garbage cans for his or her stuff.

Cleaning

Set aside a certain evening or afternoon or morning every week when the household will do a general cleaning. Even if you have a cleaning person come in, you will need to unclutter your home before it can be cleaned by an outsider. This sweep shouldn't take long if everyone has been chipping in throughout the week, not allowing rooms to become too cluttered.

Cleaning day should be on a fixed schedule so that one person in the household is not constantly nagging everyone else when it's time to do their share. If someone misses the general cleaning, that person should do more than their share the next week.

For daily tasks, each person should have set assignments. Sit down and talk it out—maybe you hate doing the dishes but don't mind doing the laundry. Both spouses should be conscientious in performing their tasks. According to a study in the mid-1990s, men did fifteen minutes of housework a week, while women generally did more than eighty minutes of cleaning.

YOUNG CHILDREN

You don't want to nag your children, but you also don't want to keep picking up after them. So what are the alternatives?

Children can be taught organizational skills, and the younger they start, the better off they will be. Even when your child is a toddler, make picking up the toys an end-of-the-day ritual. It can signal that bedtime is near and help create a pattern that makes sending kids to bed easier.

Make putting things away as easy as possible. Get a toy box that a child can open and reach into. An adjustable tension rod is a handy way to make hanging clothes easy for children, and it can be adjusted as the children grow. Encourage your children from the time they are toddlers to put their own clothes in the hamper.

Toy Storage

If your children always play in the living room, put the toy storage there—even if it is also the room used for entertaining. An attractive box is a better alternative to having games and action figures scattered across the floor.

If your children routinely play with their toys in a certain area, put the toy storage there. For that matter, if they toss their clothes in one particular spot, then put a hamper in that spot. That way you won't have to fight their old habits. Later, after your children have acquired the habit of putting their things away you can shift the storage container to a different spot.

If the majority of play takes place in the bedroom, arrange a corner for toy and game storage as well as creative supplies. Place the proper size chairs and tables there so children can sit and play comfortably.

Children should be allowed to keep special projects out on the table or in a designated spot in their room. For example, a dollhouse or racetrack could be left set up for weeks on end if these items are regularly played with. However, the rest of the floor should be cleared of toys and games every day before the child goes to bed.

A single large storage box is not necessarily the best way to store toys. The toys become jumbled and difficult to find. Stackable bins, low shelves, drawers, or cabinets are more effective.

Keep smaller "like" toys together in containers. It helps if the containers are clear plastic so you can see the toys inside. That way you won't have to take time labeling the container and your children will be able to identify where the toy they want is.

When one of your children get a new game or toy, make it part of the fun of getting something new to find a place where it will be stored. Are they blocks that go in the blocks container? Or a small plush puppet that goes in the stuffed-animal container? Let the child learn for himself that like things go together.

Uncluttering

When it is time to clean the room, prompt your child to see the scattered toys and clothing as objects that have their proper place. Ask her to fetch all the big toys or games first and put them in their place. Then gather the smaller toys into their containers. Then the books. Then the creative supplies. Then the clothes. This categorizes the things in the child's mind rather than forcing her to do the more daunting task of working systematically from the door to the bed.

Set clear standards for cleaning and try to be consistent. Does the blanket have to be folded every day? Can the craft supplies and containers of Play-doh stay on the table? Does the child get to sleep with one or two or three stuffed animals?

Keep cleaning tasks suited to the child's age. When a child is very young, you can help with the cleaning, but as the child gets older, his responsibilities should increase. Make a game of cleaning or tell a familiar story or sing the child's favorite song while you do it. This will create good associations with cleaning clutter for the child.

Kids have lots of paper clutter. Teach them how to rotate the art projects displayed on the refrigerator. When a new one comes home, it is admired and pinned up with a magnet, while the old one cheerfully goes in the trash. You can keep one or two art projects a year and save them in a special file in your file cabinet.

With school papers, admire the good grades and post them on the refrigerator (rotating the papers just like the art). The not-so-good ones can be discussed and thrown in the trash, while making a commitment to study more for the next test.

The most important school papers should be filed along with your important papers. Show your children where their school transcripts, health information, and saved art projects go. Then they will learn your good filing habits.

The best way to teach your child how to keep clutter from taking over your household is by example. Both parents should work to keep the house clutter-free, and they should include the children in that process as much as possible.

Eliminating Children's Clutter

Helping children learn when it is time to get rid of unused or old possessions prevents another clutter collector from joining the population. Approach elimination with the idea that "things" are cyclical, like summer into fall into winter into spring and back into summer again. Teach them that possessions are in your life for a while, then at some point they go away.

If a child resists throwing or giving something away, never force the issue. Explain your own system of putting objects away in a box so you can look at them later and decide if you want to keep them.

You can create an active "think about it" space where toys or games that the child is considering getting rid of are gathered. Let the child decide what goes when you point out they haven't played with his Lincoln Logs or Magna-Doodle in the past year.

If there are toys and games that are only rarely played with, store them for a few months. Then bring them out again. It will add novelty to the toy and if the child still doesn't play with it, he will more readily give it up because it's not as familiar. If the child hesitates about throwing the toy away, put it in the active "think about it" play area.

Children can be worse pack rats than adults because meaning is invested in their possessions that parents may not know about or understand. Don't create a lifetime pack rat by being too pushy about your children throwing away their belongings. As they grow up, the naturally discard things they are "too old" to play with.

TEENAGERS

Things change when your children reach adolescence. Sometimes a child will become ultra-neat, while most others live in continual disorder. Hopefully you've instilled some clutter consciousness in them that will survive puberty.

If your teenager perenially keeps a cluttered room, the

cause may be something other than a lack of organizational skills or cleanliness. Teenagers don't like to be told what to do with themselves or their possessions. Complicating this, their privacy is of utmost importance.

If you can deal with it, simply tell your teenager to keep his or her door closed. Insist on a once a month sweep just for family health. If you're consistent, they won't put up too much of a fuss—after all, once a month is not a lot to ask. Once a week is even better.

It's not a good idea to clean the rooms of teenagers. They will never be faced with the consequences of their lack of effort if you do it for them. Besides, most older teenagers really don't want their parents in their rooms or drawers or closets, and parents should respect that. It's part of growing up and moving out from under the protective parental umbrella.

PETS

You wouldn't think a dog or cat could collect so much clutter in their short lifetimes, but they do. Anything from old beds, leashes, collars, bowls, to a little raincoat that seemed like such a cute idea at the time.

Throw away old toys that are no longer played with. Get rid of most toys that were never favorites and still seem new. Get rid of the cushion they rarely sleep on or the dog house they don't use.

Beware of pet-care products gathering in your garage or utility room. Throw out old half-empty shampoo, and old shedding combs and brushes. Pet medicine also goes bad, so don't keep worming medicine or vitamin supplements for longer than a year.

Pet clutter can get mixed up with anything in your house. Designate one drawer or shelf to your pet supplies and gradually, as you're decluttering your home, you'll find those nail clippers that went missing two years ago. You'll find collars you never knew you had or biscuits that were never opened.

Helpful Hints

- Ask your housemates to commit themselves to leaving a room in better shape than they found it.
- Each person needs his or her own private space, including work space, closet space, and storage space.
- Cleaning day should be on a fixed schedule so that one person in the household is not constantly nagging everyone else when it's time to do their share.
- Children can be taught organizational skills, and the younger they start, the better.
- When your child gets a new game or toy, make it part of the fun of getting something new to find where it gets put away.
- Don't clean your teenager's room. In addition to invading her privacy, you are depriving her the experience of learning from her actions.
- Beware of pet-care products and supplies gathering in drawers and shelves.

5 : *Storage* : *Solutions*

Most of your possessions are stored until it is time to use them. This chapter deals with the basics of clearing out and organizing shelves, closets, drawers, and other storage areas.

When you're going through your storage areas to clean them out and reorganize them, start with the most inaccessible shelf or drawer and work your way toward the most accessible. You should start in the back because the useless stuff naturally gravitates to the back. With closets, start in the back corner and work your way forward. By starting in the most inaccessible spot, you'll come across objects that are long forgotten and never used. These things can be immediately thrown away with hardly a pang of loss. You'll get instant satisfaction at seeing progress being made so quickly.

This method also gives you room to shuffle objects around and see what you really use. Most people make the mistake of starting at the most accessible spot where the useful objects have gathered. Of course you will want to keep most of these things, and that will discourage you from going any further.

Make sure to pick up each object and ask yourself if you use it. If you don't, or if you hear yourself answer, "But I might need this someday…" or "This is a perfectly good _____…," throw it out or put it in a box to take to Goodwill. If you haven't used it because you didn't know you had it or couldn't find it, then it needs to be stored in a more visible spot.

Have a box waiting for objects you're not sure about. Store these for a year. When you check them after a year, you'll probably throw them away. Only include the things you can't part with but know you should throw away in this box. Don't move all your clutter into "wait and see" boxes because you'll just have to throw it all out next year.

WHERE DOES EVERYTHING GO?

You will probably need to reorganize the things you decide to keep. Ask yourself two important questions to determine where to store these items: 1) How often is the object used? 2) Where is it used?

The more frequently you use something, the more accessible it should be. Ideally, all frequently used objects should be stored in the handiest places, the places where they're used.

Things that aren't used often—maps, reference books, candles, a magnifying glass—should have their own storage place as well that don't have to be as easily accessible as frequently used items.

Larger things that you don't use very often—sewing machine, typewriter, electric blanket, fan—should be stored in an out-of-the-way place, either a low shelf or on a rack in the back of the closet. Try to keep these things together so that you'll automatically go to that spot when you need a large item you don't use often. If you scatter these possessions among your active objects, they will become clutter.

At some point, you'll find yourself surrounded by objects that have no clearly defined category and no relation to other miscellaneous objects. Don't just clump them together into the first space you find; this will defeat your purpose of organizing your things so you can find them easily. Instead, consider the use of each object. Binoculars are generally used outside of the house, so a closet or shelf near the door or in the garage is a good location for them and other outdoorsy items like a cooler or tent.

Keep similar objects together, similar in use and frequency of use. If you vacuum your living room more often than your bedroom, put the vacuum in the closet nearest the living room. If you use the hand-vacuum on the kitchen floor, keep it in the kitchen. Sounds easy, right: all office supplies in one drawer, and all your underwear in another. If it's so easy, why do you have a junk drawer? If you must have a junk drawer, go through it once a year. Throw out most of the stuff that has accumulated there and put the rest where it really belongs.

CLOSETS

Evaluate each closet in your home. What will you be storing in each—game, linen, supplies, clothes? Do the closets have shelves? Depending on how the shelves are spaced, how can you make maximum use of the closet? Is the closet in a useful area of the house for its intended storage purpose? If you're storing children's games, they should be within the child's reach—and not taller. A linen closet should be close to bedrooms and bathrooms. The pantry should be next to the kitchen.

How you store your things depends on how often you use them. Clear plastic bins, jars, and open baskets are practical alternatives. These types of storage containers should be used for frequently needed items and kept on the most handy shelves.

When storing your possessions for an extended period of time, boxes are the most convenient receptacles. Take the time to clearly label the box with its contents on the top and on at least two sides. Go through your boxes once a year and throw out things you don't use—knickknacks, clothes, gifts. This is a good time to rotate your decorations. If there's nothing in storage you would rather have on display in your home, why are you keeping all that junk. Throw away your old things to make room for new ones. This also allows you to look at the possessions you have with new appreciation.

Eliminating Closet Clutter

Chose one closet to start with. You won't need anything but large garbage bags. If you've decided that the hall closet should hold general family storage such as tool-boxes, electronic equipment, photo albums, and games, begin organizing that closet by removing all the kitchen, bedroom, and home office stuff currently occupying it.

Take a cursory look at the things that are visible and remove the things that don't belong. Immediately take these things to the places where they will ultimately be stored. Look around the house for anything that could be moved into general family storage and bring it to this closet. Don't pull everything out at once or start fitting things in before everything has been evaluated.

Once you've assessed what is visible, go to the deepest, highest corner and pull out the boxes or things you've stored up there. Ten to one you don't use anything on the top shelf. Hold the object in your hands and ask yourself: "Have I used this in the past year? Ever?" Then why are you holding on to it? Refer to chapter 1 if you need to reassure yourself that you can let go of things without guilt or panic.

If you can think of specific instances in the past year when you needed this object, move it to a more convenient and noticeable place. Perhaps if you store it with like things, it will be easier to find.

Go through all the boxes on the top shelf. If you have used an object in the past year, it can be returned to that shelf unless it needs to be handier. Some boxes of stuff may need to be shifted into a different storage area. Have a box available as a catchall to semi-sort the objects you pull from the closet until they can be stored in their proper place.

Once you've cleared the shelf and thrown away everything you don't use, you will have more space to work with. Move to the next shelf and start at the most inaccessible corner. The bottom shelf should be reserved for the heaviest things.

When at all possible, keep like things together: bowling ball, bag, and shoes; projector and boxes of slides. Don't stack loose objects on top of one another, and only stack boxes two high.

GARAGE, BASEMENT, AND ATTIC

Entire rooms devoted to storage present special problems. These areas should be clearly delineated from your living space. Junk that gathers in these rooms can molder for years and years. This is where the expensive stuff is kept that you don't want to get rid of: exercise equipment, old TVs, clothes, and furniture. The junk you don't need is mixed in with the good stuff you use: lumber, luggage, and tools to name a few.

Just because you have an attic, basement, or garage doesn't mean you need to fill it with useless stuff. The same rule applies to these storage rooms as any other areas of your home: If you don't use it, don't keep it. Keeping something because it may come in handy someday is just a cop-out for not letting go.

Do a big clutter sweep of each of your storage rooms once a year. Plan to get rid of 50 percent of what's stored there. Then, if you do even half of that, you're way ahead. Give things away that you always intended to give away. Throw away those old children's toys and books or give them to young relatives or a day-care center.

Only keep packing boxes for a week or two after you purchase an item. Don't hang on to "original" boxes just because something came in them. When you move, you'll have to order dozens of boxes anyway—it's worth it to order another dozen instead of wasting space with old cartons for years.

Go through those automotive supplies, the lawn and garden equipment, paintbrushes and cans, whatever you've got. Throw out the duplicates and the outdated supplies. Organize like things together on shelves or in cabinets. Get rid of broken flowerpots, old furniture, torn window screens, rusted pipe, leftover shingles—anything that you don't have a use for right now is clutter. Throw out the old swing set, the croquet set nobody plays with, and the hammock you never use.

Also, toss out scraps, like the end of the roll of wallpaper, extra carpeting from your living room, short lengths of cable or chain, vinyl floor tiles, and near-empty cans of paint unless the carpet or wallpaper is one-of-a-kind custom made. You can't do anything with a scrap and keeping it around is just wasting space.

If you have to hold on to them, keep pesticides, fertilizers, and toxic cleaners together in one secured area, even if there aren't any children around. Most of these things should be thrown away because toxic substances cause a large number of household accidents, yet many people keep cans and jars of stuff that have only a few inches of a product in them—not enough to do a job, but enough to seriously harm someone if they swallowed it or got it on their skin. Purchase these on an as-needed basis.

CREATING NEW STORAGE SPACES

Sometimes people get excited about clearing out clutter and their first impulse is to go out and buy new shelves, trunks, and file cabinets, but eliminating clutter should come first; organization second. Often, if you eliminate the things you don't use, you'll find you have plenty of space to organize the rest. If you work the other way, you'll end up with rooms jam-packed with neatly organized and categorized clutter—not to mention more pieces of furniture taking up what could be available space. But you still won't be able to find anything and you'll have paid to store stuff you don't use. Once you've gone through all your things and thrown away as much as you can, assess your storage space. If you find you don't have enough storage then, it's time to add more.

Sometimes a clutter problem is really a space problem. When you don't have enough separate storage room for everything your things get jumbled. Then you aren't using things because you can't find them.

When you're looking for new storage space, don't zoom in on those small spaces between things, like the area between your couch and the wall or between file cabinets. Don't fill every niche with stuff. The beauty of getting rid of clutter is discovering and cherishing the space around things. Think of these spaces as frames setting off a piece of furniture or object.

Think creatively when you're looking for new storage space. Bookshelves can accommodate things other than books: Place smaller things in baskets or boxes so the shelf still looks attractive. Your antique hope chest can be filled with linen or out-of-season clothing. If your files only fill one drawer in your cabinet, use the other to store office supplies.

A wide variety of manufactured organizers are available to store your things: shoe trees, stackable hatboxes, cabinets with drawers, bins with trays, and more. Look through a catalog, or walk through the aisles of storage containers in your local home-improvement store, or in a specialty store that sells organizers. But don't buy anything right away. Take a look at what's offered, then go home and see what sort of space you have compared with what you need to store. That beige satin organizer might have looked great in the store, but looking at your closet, you may realize you need the heavy-duty canvas organizer with the sixteen pockets instead of eight. Only then should you go back and make your purchases.

Shelves

A good place to build shelves is in a closet. Then you won't have to worry about having unsightly things stored in plain view. If it's a child's closet, make the shelves strong enough so a child can step on them or lean on one while reaching for a higher shelf.

In a walk-in closet, line all three walls with shelves. In sliding-door closets, line the long wall with shelves, placing a support in the middle so you can store heavier objects. Don't shelve in the entire space: Leave space in front for floor-to-ceiling items like fishing rods or skis.

If space permits, add another shelf above the one you already have in your closet, doubling your space. Or put a narrow row of shelves up one side and install a second bar to double-hang shirts. You can also buy bars that hang directly from the clothes bar, which are adjustable.

In small rooms, especially the pantry or utility room, build shelves supported by floor-to-ceiling posts. Or, put a narrow row of shelves in the closet. This dramatically increases the potential use of these storage rooms. If possible, install adjustable shelves. Then store items of the same height on the same shelf. You can also add more shelves later if you need to.

For larger rooms, you can include a wide bookcase that juts into the room, creating a niche for a desk or table. Use both sides of the bookcase for book and basket storage. If you can't go to the trouble to hang shelves or purchase or build a bookcase—if you rent an apartment or you haven't got the time or money—place a chest of drawers in the closet. The top can be stacked with boxes.

In the bedroom or the kitchen, a shelf just below the ceiling all around the room is a decorative way to store items not used frequently. In a child's room, stuffed animals as well as dolls or figurines can be displayed

Newer homes sometimes have built-in "pot shelves" where you can place plants and decorative items. Try to keep plants off the top of tables and desks. If you have a lot of plants, you can build shelves in the window frame itself. Plants can also be hung from a ceiling hook with a butterfly bolt, or from a triangle hinge attached to the wall.

Hanging Things

Hooks placed on the backs of doors are a convenient method of hanging things. You use a space that is currently going to waste, and it keeps the hanging objects out of sight.

In your private bathroom, you can hang nightgowns, pajamas, and bathrobes on the back of the door. Outdoor clothing can be hung on the inside of a closet door near the entryway. Shoes or accessories can be put in a flat shoe tree that hangs on the inside of the closet door in your bedroom.

If you don't have enough door space, place hooks on the side walls of your closets to hang your camera, purses, carrybags, umbrellas, or what have you. On the walls in your workroom or den, hang speakers, fans, photographs, awards, racks or shelves.

In New York City, where space is severely limited, many people hang things from the ceiling or high on the wall, including exercise equipment, bicycles, folding chairs or tables, musical instruments. I've seen apartments where you have to walk through a hallway hung with a person's possessions before you reach the living room. Try to restrict this sort of hanging to a utility room or small storage room if you have the space available and not one of the frequently used rooms of the house.

New Possessions

When you bring something new into your home or office, decide immediately where it will be stored. Don't assume it will fall into the right place automatically. That will only ensure that your new possession will sit around indefinitely until you stop seeing it in the general clutter. You may eventually have to move it to a place that is more convenient, but that's better than leaving it out. Figure out where you will most often use the item, and store it nearby.

Knowing that you have to store things as soon as you bring them home can help you avoid adding clutter to your life. If you know you have to find a place for it, and you can't think of where or how you'll use this item in the next few months, simply don't bring it home.

Helpful Hints

- Store objects according to how accessible and convenient they need to be.
- Where is the object used? Store it in a place near where it is used.
- Make certain that each closet suits your storage needs.
- While clearing clutter from a closet, have a box or two ready to act as a catchall, so you can semi-sort the objects until they can be stored in their proper place.
- Organize your existing storage and eliminate clutter before adding new storage.
- A good place to build shelves is in a closet.
- Decide where a new possession will be stored as soon as you bring it into the house.

6 : *Clothing Clutter*

You can spend hundreds of dollars on a wardrobe makeover, but your efforts will be for naught if your useful clothes get lost in the clutter. This chapter deals with clothing and accessories: how to sort them, how to store them, and when to get rid of them. If you've ever found a piece of clothing you forgot you had, or couldn't find something you wanted to wear, you probably need to eliminate some clothing clutter. If you can find a garment you would have worn if you had seen it, then it's time to eliminate some clothing clutter.

Don't let the thought of how much money you spent on your clothing stop you from getting rid of some of it. Every piece of clothing you own will eventually get worn out anyway and have to be disposed of.

Get rid of it even if it's a fairly new garment or something that you've never even worn. The money has already been wasted—keeping a reminder of that waste in your closet is not going to bring the money back.

Clothing clutter interferes with a working wardrobe

because clothes can easily become lost or they get wrinkled and you won't wear them because they have to be ironed. You might not see the possibilities in your wardrobe because you're too busy ignoring those pants that are too small for you or that skirt you don't like because it's too short—even though you love the color.

Keep in mind that nearly half of everyone's wardrobe consists of clothes they never wear. You could throw half your clothes out right now, today, and never miss them. You will, however, enjoy the spaciousness of your closet and appreciate your wardrobe because everything in it is something you like to wear.

SORTING CLOTHES

As in any clutter-elimination ceremony, start with the most inaccessible drawer or the furthest hanger in your closet. Look at the clothes you don't wear. Why are you keeping them? Do they still fit, but you hate the style, or do you love the style and color, but are yourself waiting to shrink to the right size? If a jacket fits perfectly but you swore you'd never wear orange again, throw it out. If you hate horizontal stripes, nothing will induce you to put on that blue-striped shirt—even if it is brand-new and a gift, to boot. Get rid of it.

Some people keep entire wardrobes in different sizes. If you've been waiting to lose ten pounds for the past ten years so you can fit in that skirt, give the skirt away. Maybe by throwing out all those skinny clothes, you can shock yourself into reality. Either live with the way you are, or make a serious effort to exercise and lose weight. Sometimes, however, people keep clothes of different sizes because their size fluctuates over the year. As long as you wear all the clothes over the course of the year, your wardrobe is viable.

Examining and evaluating your wardrobe once a year is the best way to stay on top of your clothes clutter. Each year you'll have the benefit of last year's efforts to build on. Eventually, it will become second nature to decide when to get rid of a garment.

People with seasonal wardrobes and small closets store their out-of-season clothes in drawers, boxes, or trunks. It's often easier to get motivated when you're examining the clothes just coming into season. You've got more at stake in having things you can wear. You also haven't seen them in a while and may have a new perspective on them.

When examining your wardrobe, try on the clothes you haven't worn in a while to properly evaluate each one. Once the garment is on, you may be surprised to remember why you never wear that sweaterdress or those cuffed pants. Have a large garbage bag ready for the castoffs so you can immediately put these clothes out of sight.

When you try on your clothes, even when you think you know what they look like, you might be surprised to find clothing you haven't worn in a while goes perfectly with your new whatever. With the clutter clothes removed, the valuable ones will be more visible.

The hardest clothing to get rid of is that which reminds you of something or someone. You may never want to wear tie-dye again, but you might not be able to part with your

Grateful Dead T-shirts. But these clothes need to be worn to remind you of those good times. Besides, it's not the clothes that are really important, but your memories. You don't need to prove to anyone that you once wore a size six or had jeans with a twenty-eight-inch waist. Who cares? Get rid of them.

Some special clothing isn't meant to be worn again, like your wedding dress. Real clothing mementos like this, including your father's Navy uniform, or an heirloom christening gown, should be carefully boxed and packed away.

If you have a special shirt or a favorite dress that you once loved and often wore, but is now no longer wearable, stiffen your spine and toss it in the trash. If that's to painful a notion, give it to a younger relative or a thrift shop.

Anything you're not sure about, box up. But look through the box in one year. Get ready for a ride down memory lane. You'll have forgotten some things, and will remember others. Most often you'll simply say, "I liked this shirt." But that doesn't change the fact that you wouldn't or couldn't or don't wear it now. Try to see these garments as clutter rather than the treasured possessions you thought they were a year ago.

Clothes that need to be mended or altered should be put in a special place. Leaving them hanging in the closet or folded in drawers will give you the illusion that they are ready to be worn. Keep these clothes with your sewing kit on a handy shelf or in a bag by the door until they can be attended to. However, if you don't take action on these clothes within a few months, throw them out.

If you're not sure you like a garment—it fits but you don't wear it often enough—put it at the end of each section of clothes where you can easily see it. That way, the option of wearing it is always under consideration. If a year rolls around and you still haven't worn it, throw it away.

Whether you recycle these clothes, donate them to a thrift shop, or throw them away, they should be removed from your home immediately. If the bag lingers for a few days on the floor of your closet, throw it away. Recycling is best, but if you're using inaction as an excuse to save clutter, don't bother.

STORING CLOTHES

Clothes you currently wear should be stored in closets, drawers, and on shelves. If your wardrobe is well-organized, you can tell with a glance what your options are.

Drawers are used for sweaters, underwear, socks, T-shirts, sweatpants, sweatshirts, nightwear, shorts, tank tops—generally, items that don't crush or crease. Store these according to the season and use. For example, put T-shirts in one drawer, shorts and tank tops in another, and underwear and socks in yet another. Shelves can be used for bulkier clothes, like sweaters.

Hang as many clothes as possible, and in sections. Within each section, organize the individual clothes according to use: evening dresses versus work dresses, long-sleeved shirts versus short-sleeved. You can further break down the sections by hanging work shirts together and golf shirts together. Don't hang pants with shirts or shirts with skirts, and so on. If you do, you'll be cheating yourself of all the possibilities your wardrobe has to offer.

Sort the sections according to how often you wear different types of clothes. The preferred clothes should be the most accessible.

This sounds like more trouble than it is. Once you have your clothes sorted, empty hangers will mark where the clothes go after they are cleaned. The system maintains itself.

Don't keep clothes that are a smaller or a larger size mixed in with the clothes that fit. Having them among your wearables will just mislead you into thinking they are available to be worn. After a while, your eyes will skim over them anyway, and you'll lose the benefit of their presence.

If you're like most people, you probably take off your clothes at night and toss them somewhere. Pick one place to be your toss pile. Whether it's the hamper, a chair, on a rack in the closet, or even one spot on the floor. Anything to keep the used clothing together. Clothes you've worn but that aren't dirty can be hung up inside out as a reminder to wash them the next time you wear them.

ACCESSORIES

To be useful, accessories need to be stored so you can see them. Jewelry should be laid out in boxes or hung on trees or boards. Jumbled jewelry is clutter. Use the same criteria to sort useful jewelry from the clutter. If you haven't worn a bracelet in years, but you're keeping it because it used to be your favorite, it's clutter now. Throw it away. If you're keeping a necklace your friend gave to you even though you would never wear it, then take it to a thrift shop so someone who will love it can buy it and wear it.

Belts and scarves can be hung up or placed in drawers. There are some interesting organizers that can hold your accessories. If you prefer using drawers, you can either compartmentalize the drawers, or fold and lay out the scarves and belts in rows so you can see them.

If you have shelf space, put your accessories in stackable clear plastic bins. That way, you can see the accessories at the same time you're looking at your clothes. And if you can see what you have, you'll know what you aren't using.

Get into the habit of returning accessories to their proper place when you undress. Cleaning up takes longer when you're picking up belts and shoes along with dirty clothes. When your things have easily accessible storage places, it's easier to return them to where they came from.

SHOES

Follow the yearly examination and sorting procedure with your shoes. Try on every pair at least once a year. Put the shoes you don't wear very often in a prominent place, within easy reach. If you still don't wear them after a year, question why you're keeping them. You may want to keep those four-inch heels for a special party, but why keep those flats that you don't really like?

Shoe collecting can be an addiction for some people. I've seen closets outfitted with shoe racks to accommodate a hundred pairs of shoes. When the shoes are organized and well-tended, it's a real collection. But remember that shoes are meant to be worn. If a pair of shoes no longer fits you, or your don't like wearing them, then don't keep them.

If you have dozens of pairs of shoes jumbled on the floor of your closet, it's time to get organized. A shoe tree is inexpensive and will quickly arrange your shoes. They won't get scuffed or bent and you'll never have to search for a shoe again.

You can buy shoe trees that sit on the floor of your closet, allowing room for heavier boots to sit underneath. Some people prefer the shoe trees with pockets that hang from the back of the door or from the clothes rack. Remember that a hanging shoe tree is inherently more flimsy than a floor rack. Before you buy anything, consider which you'd prefer while you're getting dressed or putting away your shoes.

BUYING CLOTHES

One way to prevent clothing clutter is to know what is in your wardrobe before you go shopping. Plan out what you like and need—colors and styles—before you enter a mall or boutique. Buying things aimlessly leads to quantities of clothing that people never wear.

Take a serious look through your wardrobe. Identify the garments you wear most often. Why? is it the color? The style? The material? Keep this in mind when you go shopping. If you love your boat-necked black sweater, you should take another look at that boat-necked blue sweater that's on sale. If you always reach for shirts with vertical pin strips first, keep an eye out for them. But that doesn't mean you have to duplicate your favorite clothes. Go for a different color, or a different material, or slightly different style.

Coordination is the key to success with your wardrobe. Certain colors look best with your skin and hair coloring. In neutral light, find out if you look best in warm or cool tones, in vibrant colors or pastels. That way, when you go to a department store with unreliable lighting, you will know which tones work for you and which ones don't.

Make color your first guideline when buying clothes. Stick to your colors even if you find something in the perfect size, style, and material. If yellow washes out your features, you won't look good no matter how well the garment fits. If browns, beiges, and rusts look great on you, resist buying a royal-blue jacket. Wait until you find one in your color—then it will suit you perfectly.

Helpful Hints

- Don't keep clothing you don't like even if it still fits— or clothing you are waiting to shrink into.
- It's often easier to get motivated when you're examining the clothes just coming into season.
- Many clothes with special memories can be kept if they are still worn, otherwise throw them out.
- Pack wedding dresses, christening gowns, and like garments carefully away.
- If you haven't worn a piece of clothing for the past year

because you couldn't find it or didn't remember you owned it, put it in a more accessible place.

- To be useful, accessories need to be stored so you can see them.
- Follow the same yearly examination and sorting procedure with your accessories and shoes as you do with your clothing.
- Make color your first priority when buying clothes.

7 : Home : Entertainment

Many people just give up when it comes to their books, videos, or music clutter. If your CDs are organized on a rack and your videos are stored so you can read the titles, congratulations. Most people aren't so organized.

The way to store these items is by following the first step you would take in organizing everything. If you just jumble your CDs or books on shelves, stacking them in random piles rather than standing them vertically, you're not going to be able to see what you have.

Slightly different techniques apply to sorting books, music, and videos than for other kinds of household clutter. You may not reference a book or watch a movie for two or three years, but that doesn't mean you throw it away. If your library is properly organized, and you've gotten rid of all the stuff you've grown out of watching or listening to, you won't lose sight of the fine options you have.

BOOKS

Most people don't think of clutter in their bookshelves, but it's there. If you buy books and don't weed out the ones you never read or use, eventually you will own more bookshelves or stacks or boxes of books than anything else. Uncluttering your bookshelves is a big task. Don't rush through it and don't worry if you have to leave boxes or piles of books out for a few days. The end result will be worth it.

Don't organize each bookshelf separately. Before you begin, evaluate your collection. If some of your books are still boxed, go through the boxes. Consider whether you are seriously going to weed out books as you go along, or if you'll be adding another bookcase.

Form categories for your library according to the types of books you own. Take a look at roughly how many books you have that fall into each category:

Art	History
Biography	How-to
Business	Psychology
Child Care	Reference
Cooking	Religious/Metaphysical
Fiction	Self-improvement
Gardening	Sports
Health	Travel

Store the books that go in each section together. For example, keep all the reference books—dictionaries, encyclopedias, atlases, maps, thesauri, quotation books, directories, almanacs—in one place for easy access. If you don't own many books, many of these sections can be joined together: psychology next to child care, self-improvement with how-to.

Split categories with the most books into subsections. Fiction can be divided into classics and mysteries, and art according to artist, period, or region. You might also arrange books by author.

Sorting and Storing Books

Don't pull all your books out at once. Instead, shuffle books around on the shelves as you go along. Sections will grow, and be exactly where you want them. If you want certain books to be more accessible, plan to keep that section within easy reach.

When you've developed your categories, think about where each should go. Reference books should be close to your desk, while books shelved in the home's public spaces should be of general interest. Frequency of use should be your first consideration. Your largest category of books will not necessarily be the one you reference or read the most.

Place similar categories together: biography and history, metaphysics and religion, health and self-help. Art and travel books are often oversized and should be shelved together on lower, larger shelves.

All of your books don't have to be kept in the same place. Depending on how often you use your cookbooks, you may want to keep them in the kitchen. Decorative bookends can keep a half-dozen cookbooks together and

attractively displayed on your counter. Books on car maintenance and repair can go on a shelf in the garage where
you'll need to reference them.

Don't cram your books onto shelves. Leave room for
new additions and books you've overlooked during your
first sort. If you don't leave some empty space, you'll end
up in the same place you started—new books will be piled
on top or haphazardly shelved wherever they will fit.

Don't stack books on their sides; that makes removal
difficult and messy. Make double rows of your books if
your bookcase or shelves are deep enough. Put the less-
used books in the rear.

Eliminating Book Clutter

Most books are relatively inexpensive, so they aren't something you have a lot invested in. But there are some people
who are very possessive about their books. I'm one of them.
I find it hard to get rid of any book, even a book I hated and
couldn't finish. Obviously, that's the first book that should be
thrown away. Don't keep books you don't like.

If you received a book as a gift and you've never read it
and you probably never will, get rid of it. Exchange it for
a book you prefer or give it to someone else. You might
even consider selling it to a used-book store donating it to
charity, or a school or library.

Some people maintain a section of books that they are
planning to read, but this section usually gets bigger and
bigger every year, with the categories jumbled together. If
you don't read a book a couple of months after you've

gotten it, store it with similar books so you know where to find it. Whenever you get a new book for a section, try to replace a book you've never read or referenced in the same section.

CDs and Cassettes

Organize your CDs and cassettes in much the same way as your books. Target and eliminate the clutter among your collection. Take a look at what you have and see how many titles you have in each category. Common categories include:

Ballads	New Age
Blues	Rap
Classical	Religious
Country	Rock/Pop
Folk	Show Tunes
Jazz	Spoken Word and Books on Tape

If you have a large category, break it into smaller sections. Some people set up special nostalgic sections to hold music they listened to a lot at one time.

Sorting and Storing Music

The best way to store CDs and cassettes is in specialized organizers. There's a hundred different ways to store your music depending on where you listen to it and how big your music library is.

Before buying any organizers, count how many CDs or cassettes you have. Consider how many you should get rid of. Then think about how many new titles you buy per month. Organizers have a specific number of slots, so you need to get something that will allow you to expand. When you store CDs in a portable pack, keep the case in your home organizer. That way, you can easily shift CDs in and out of your portable pack.

Frequency of use should be the first consideration when storing CDs or cassettes. The largest category of music you own may not be the one you listen to the most. Within the categories, the work of each musician, composer, or performer should be kept together. Some people alphabetize their music library according to the name or title. But if you're organizing your music library from scratch, don't worry about that right now.

Leave enough empty slots within each category to add new titles and resist the urge to mix categories by storing your most-played titles together. By placing these titles in their proper category, along with other titles by the same artist, you'll have more options to chose from when you're in the mood for that type of music.

Eliminating Music Clutter

If you have CDs or cassettes that you never listen to anymore, consider whether you want to keep them. If you know it's not likely you'll ever listen to it again, get rid of it. If you received the CD or cassette as a gift and you've never listened to it and probably never will, exchange it for something you would listen to, or give it away. Give your old cassettes and CDs to a hospital or thrift shop. Someone will get enjoyment out of the music even if you don't.

VIDEOS

Videotapes can become instant clutter, especially if you don't keep up with labeling tapes you record yourself. Many people never even watch the shows they had to tape and toss those tapes in cabinets where they lie for years.

The problem with storing videotapes flat is that the tape can shift on the spool. Then it feeds across the heads of the VCR unevenly, causing the image to deteriorate. You can sometimes fix this by fast-forwarding to the end of the tape, then rewinding. Store the video on an end, either the long one or the short end.

Store your videos in video boxes, either the one it came in or plastic boxes. Boxes keep videos from deteriorating because the tape is sensitive to moisture, dust, and light. Plastic airtight cases are inexpensive, and are the only way to preserve your tapes for more than a few years. Tapes have to be transferred after a few years, otherwise the emulsion gets scraped off by the video heads and clogs the works.

Sorting and Storing Videos

Videotapes can be categorized in the following manner:
Documentaries
Exercise
Games

Home movies
Movies
Self-help

Throw away movies you know you won't ever watch again. The same goes for exercise tapes that you no longer use. Never get rid of home movies, however. You'll almost always regret not having more footage of your loved ones. But remember to transfer the images every four or five years in order to keep them from deteriorating.

Helpful Hints

- Form categories for your library according to the types of books you own.
- Unlike most clutter, even if you don't reference a book or watch a movie for two or three years, you might keep it anyway.
- Shuffle books on the shelves as you go along; don't pull them all down at once to re-sort.
- Try to get rid of books you'll never read or reference, and books you've read but didn't like.
- The best way to store CDs and cassettes is in specialized organizers.
- Never get rid of home movies; have them re-recorded every handful of years to preserve the images.

8 : *Paper*
: *Clutter*

This section is for you if you don't like making deci-sions about what records to keep. You have to protect your important papers because paper that isn't properly taken care of collects bad reminders of where it's been: coffee stains, pen marks, smudges, soda spills, grease from your lunch, and so on. Your records will be ruined if they're not protected and preserved. You can also lose important papers among other papers if you are inundated with paper clutter.

The problem with eliminating paper clutter is we're faced with so much of it. Then, we have to read the infor-mation on each and every sheet and determine if it is valu-able enough to keep—a more difficult task than evaluating and downsizing knickknacks or duplicates. But the guide-lines for eliminating paper clutter are just as easy to follow as they are with other overflow.

You may be tempted to throw out the whole mound of paper stacked on your desk or stored in your filing cabinets and boxes. But that will never teach you the process of keeping paper flowing through your office. Plus, as you go through the papers, you'll inevitable find things you need, and information that is important. That will teach you how to quickly recognize the few pieces of wheat among the chaff, and it will become easier to maintain a clutter-free office.

The relief of going through a pile of papers is worth far more than the fifteen or twenty minutes it took to make those decisions. You spend far more time than that every week worrying about everything you have to get done, and working around that huge pile.

PAPER-CLUTTER TRAPS

A bulletin board can be a bad idea if it's not maintained. It often becomes a catchall for things that aren't important, obscuring the urgent message. To keep a bulletin board useful, messages should be removed once they are received, and out-of-date information should be thrown away every day. Papers shouldn't overlap because that defeats the purpose of displaying them.

Another deceptive clutter trap is the "to read" pile. You put things there to take care of on an undefined "someday." But that day usually never comes. Those old piles of newspapers, magazines, catalogs, newsletters, and clippings should be dealt with then thrown away immediately.

A classic clutter trap is a work seminar. You return with booklets, notes, advertising sheets, folders, etc. Most of it you won't ever use again. Separate any information you may need to act on, or file the contact information in your Rolodex or electronic organizer, and throw away the rest.

Rough drafts are also clutter traps. Just because they were necessary to the creation of a project or memo doesn't mean you need to hold on to them. Only the final product should be kept, otherwise you might mistake the rough draft for the final version.

Any outdated paper should be thrown away: expired coupons, loose receipts more than a year old, expired leases, old bankbooks, and so on. Also any stationery, envelopes, business cards, stamps, order forms, or deposit slips saving outdated pages for "scratch paper," you probably don't use enough scratch paper to make it worth your while. Besides, someone could accidentally use these official-looking papers. Also, throw away old notebooks. Those notes may have been important at one time, but people rarely refer back to an old notebook.

TIPS TO PREVENT PAPER CLUTTER

One thing that will help to reduce paper clutter is to clean up after you've finished working on something. Throw away the papers you don't need, file the ones that are important, and get rid of extra copies and previous revisions. If you leave it for later, your project is not truly completed. Later you'll be tempted to shove the pile away or file all the documents when half should have been thrown out when you were done. Make time to finish. If you deal with each piece of paper while it is fresh on your mind, you won't have to touch it again.

A great way to eliminate paper clutter is to use only one calendar to record appointments and deadlines. When recording projects or appointments, write down the most pertinent information—time, address, phone number, name, and directions as you get them. Don't write it on a post-it, then transfer it to your book. Keep a record of everything in one date book. Keep a rolodex, address book, an electronic organizer, or handheld PC with all you contact information in it. If you routinely collect business cards, you can also buy business-card holders. These are flip files with a holder for each card. Sales professionals tend to carry these because you can easily slip a card in or out. For other people, it's a lot of bulk when you can simply input the information into your address book or organizer. Put all your notes and ideas in one notebook or folder. If you routinely gather bits of paper, buy manila folders that have only one open end.

Always throw out last month's magazine and yesterday's newspaper when the new one arrives. Even if you haven't read it, the periodical already had its chance. If you find yourself throwing out a magazine month after month without looking at it, don't renew the subscription.

Don't keep old copies of magazines around the house. Many people subscribe to a trade magazine for their business, and after they read it, they carefully stack it somewhere with all the others. Throw these away. If you really need some information, you will find it much easier on the Internet or in the library.

SORTING AND STORING PAPER

There are four ways to process a piece of paper so it doesn't join the piles on your desk or floor. With each piece of paper that comes across your desk, you need to decide how you're going to deal with it:

- Act on it
- Throw it away
- Refer it to someone
- File it for reference

Act On It

Documents that require action take precedence. They should be filed in a project folder stored in an accessible location. Write down what you have to do. A note on a pad that lists everything you have to do is much easier to keep track of than anonymous pieces of paper lying in piles. You'll know at a glance what needs to be done. Then, when it's time to do the job, the folder will have all the information you gathered.

Beware of to do folders. Only keep one if you're also writing down what needs to be done. Otherwise, you might forget that action needs to be taken. The good thing about a to-do folder is that it can serve as a catchall for papers that don't have their own folder. As you go through your to do folder, see if there are papers that can be filed together, forming a new project folder.

Project folders can be transitory. Once a project is finished, you don't need to keep the support or reference material. Those papers can be thrown away, the folder flipped and reused for the next project.

If a piece of paper has contact information on it (names, phone numbers, etc.), then immediately write it in your book or record it in your organizer. Then throw away the piece of paper. Loose notes can be transferred to your datebook or calendar.

For some correspondence, you don't need to write it in a computer and print it out, just write a note on notepaper and send it right off. Or start the outline of a project, and plan on expanding it later. File the outline and you'll be glad to have something down you start working with.

Throw Away

When in doubt, save tax, legal, and financial documents. This doesn't mean every receipt or check stub, but documents that contain necessary information (this will be covered in-depth under "Filing").

It should be easy to throw a lot of your paper clutter away: Fed Ex receipts, memos, old phone messages, coupons, grocery lists, to do lists, junk mail, Post-it notes, and so on.

Throw away copies and old versions of reports and memos. If you need another one, make a copy. When you make copies for distribution, make only the amount you need.

Resource information should be thrown out unless you have a use for it in a specific project. Then it should go into that project folder until it is used. After the project is done, the reference material should be thrown out unless it can be recycled in another project. If you have trouble getting rid of resource information, refer to "Information" in chapter 2.

Refer It

Paper flow sometimes gets stuck when you need an address, a check, or a confirmation phone call before the project or task is completed. Everything is on hold until you can get an answer. In- and out-boxes are best used for referring documents to other people. Use a general out-box that you distribute once a day or when it gets full. If you have one person or department that you regularly refer documents to, give them a dedicated box.

In-boxes work well for your household, too. Mail, messages, and notes can be left in each person's slot or compartment in an organizer that is stored in a general-use area.

The best use for Post-it notes is for loose papers that need to be referred to someone. The recipient's name should be clearly marked on either the document itself or on the Post-it. Your initials and the reason you're referring it to them can also be jotted down. If a phone call doesn't get you the information, then make a copy of the document and place a Post-it on it with your request. That way, the person you refer it to will have the piece of paper with the information and the reminder of what you need.

If something has to be mailed out, immediately put it in an envelop and address it. This saves the time of having to deal with this set of papers again, and it keeps the documents together and ready to go.

FILE IT

The theory of good filing is to only touch paper once. You do something with it, then you file it or throw it away. If you get used to immediately filing papers, you won't have to waste time worrying about those loose papers and rereading them to figure out where they should go. Resist the urge to keep files or papers in a box or pile on top of your desk. Get rid of the paper or file it where it belongs.

File your folders in drawers and cabinets because desktop file holders create clutter. People use them as an excuse to not clear out the clutter from their filing cabinets. Soon one file holder turns into two, or three. If you have relatively few folders, perhaps for household information, accordion folders can neatly organize your documents by year. You can have one or several folders for long-term information—mortgage, insurance, social security. Dedicate an accordion folder to money management.

However, in our paper-intensive day, almost every household needs a filing cabinet. You can buy a two-drawer cabinet for very little money, and all of your papers will be organized and at the tip of your fingers. Even if you only use one drawer for files, the other can be used for storage of photo albums, telephone books, computer disks, office supplies, instruction booklets, or stationery.

Some people delay organizing their files because they think they should have hanging folders with tabs and manila folders with typed labels, with everything alphabetized. But unless you are handling your files all day every day, manila folders with handwritten labels should suffice.

Always keep a copy of the following in a file an the original in a safe or safety deposit box: adoption papers, birth certificates, custody agreements, death certificates, deeds, divorce decrees, marriage certificates, passports, and wills.

Never throw away: health records, income tax returns, IRA records of contributions, owners manuals, and warranties.

Keep for six years: bank records, canceled checks, and credit-card records. I've been advised to keep contracts for seven years after their expiration date.

Keep for four years: insurance policies after expiration date, investment records, loan papers, mortgage papers, tax records, and utility bills.

Sorting Files

Create a filing system that keeps your records and information accessible. If you don't you'll find yourself surrounded by file clutter. Your filing system should be customized to your specific needs, tailored to your personality and type of work you do. File things in order to keep them safe, but it's even more important to be able to find them fast.

Make sure the labels are clear and easy to read. If you call your car a car, then don't label the folder "Automobile." And don't label a folder with an individual's name when you're dealing with his or her company.

For projects, don't file an article on cat health under "Cats" if the project you're working on is how to find a good veterinarian. Label the folder "Veterinarian," and don't put anything in that folder that isn't related to the project.

When filing reference information that will be accessed

for many different projects, each category should have its own folder(s) with each supplier's brochures and information.

Make your files broad enough so that they contain a number of documents. If you get a monthly statement for something, give it its own folder.

Beware of thick folders. Before splitting a folder in two, make sure you need everything in it. You will probably be able to cull outdated reference information or documents you no longer need.

File your folders according to general categories: business, financial, entertainment, and personal. Each category can be color-coded to aid in refiling and locating folders. You can file alphabetically within these sections, or with the most frequently used folders in the front.

The following are some examples of files you are likely to have in every category:

- Business
    Contacts
    Marketing
    Personnel
    Projects
    Reports
    Resumé
    Vendors
- Financial
    Banking—checking, credit cards, IRA, money-
        market account
    Contracts—prenuptial agreement, wills

Home—mortgage, rental lease
Insurance—automobile, health, home, life
Investments—bonds, pension, real estate, stocks
Loans—car, student
Taxes—receipts, yearly returns
Warranties and guaranties—product information
- Entertainment
  Consumer information
  Gift ideas
  Hobbies
  Party planners
  Restaurants—take-out menus
  Travel—car rentals, frequent-flyer miles, hotels
- Personal
  Archives—birth, passport, social-security card (could
     go under financial category)
  Automobile—maintenance, service
  Correspondence
  Health and medical information
  Home—exterminator, maintenance, repair
  Pets—medical, supplies
  Photographs—negatives
  School history

Additionally, you can make general-reference folders for each category. Consistently file your information from either the front or the back of the folder so the papers are in chronological order. If you maintain your files and cull out all but the necessary documents in each folder, it makes it easier to locate particular papers.

Note which folders you reach for the most often. These categories should be given priority closest to the front of the drawer. Keep folders for the same project together, with the most-used folder in the front of that section. Color-code files you use often with a special color or put them at the front of the drawer.

Don't pull a file until you need it. Mark down the projects you need to do in your daybook or a notepad, and only pull the folder when you're ready for it. When you're done, immediately file it again. That way you always know where it is.

STORING PAPER

Unfortunately, you documents can be filed away and stacked neatly in boxes, and it is still clutter. Everyone should go through their files once a year and clear them out. The temptation to store old papers is too great to avoid. That's why offices end up with huge storerooms of boxes that nobody ever looks at. They're filled with copies and ancient correspondence and outdated information. Why hang on to these papers?

There is a misconception that more storage room will solve your problem. But it would take a storage room the size of a landfill to hold all the paper you'll generate while you're working. You need to get rid of some of that paper.

Consider your file cabinet. Are there folders you never refer to? Support material for old projects that can be thrown out? Often the entire folder can be tossed, or at most, only the final report or product saved.

Go through folders you regularly refer to as well. There is no reason to keep every piece of paper that's in a folder simply because at one time you thought you would need it. Throw out reference material that's been replaced by new data. Throw out copies of prior versions and save only the latest working copy.

Only very important files, like financial and legal documents, should go into boxed storage. Client files may be saved for a couple of years, but sometimes that's not necessary. Never put project files into storage unless the project is not completed and won't be worked on for a year or two.

MAIL

Mail is usually a big part of paper clutter. The mail starts out as neat envelopes, but when it's opened all sorts of off-sized paper fall out. Unopened junk mail piles up.

Sort mail according to whom it is going to. Each person should have a specific place where their mail is stored in your home. As you sift through your mail, throw as much away as possible. Most junk mail should be thrown away unopened. Why bother? You didn't ask for this information, and it's usually someone trying to get money from you or sell you something. Your name is sold from company to company, and you are the constant target of marketing techniques and ploys. Don't buy into it—throw it away without a second thought.

Throw out junk that comes with your bills, too. When you open the bill, save only the bill and the return envelope. Get rid of everything else or it will become clutter.

Put the bill in your folder or slot. New catalogs can replace old ones (which should be thrown out), and business information should go in its own project folder.

Credit-card offers seem to be the most tempting, but don't keep anything unless you have a clear and immediate use for it. If you're planning on getting new car insurance, put any notices you get in your insurance folder. Don't keep "interesting" mail in a pile that's waiting to be dealt with.

Unless a letter is very special, throw away personal correspondence. You don't need to save every card your sister and grandmother sends you—unless it includes an extra-special note. If you want to save correspondence, have a folder for each person you write to. This used to be a minimal problem, but with e-mail, the return of the letter means you can quickly gather boxes of correspondence you don't really need.

Helpful Hints

- Any outdated paper should be thrown away.
- Resource information should be thrown out unless you have a use for it in a specific project.
- In- and out-boxes are used for referring documents to other people
- Resist the urge to keep files or papers in a box or piled on top of your desk.
- Don't pull a file until you need it.
- Most junk mail should be thrown away unopened.
- Unless a letter is very special, throw away personal correspondence.

9 : *Clutter-Free Office*

Your work environment should be the most efficient area in your life, yet it is often the most cluttered. Not only does clutter take up valuable space, it eats up valuable time because you have to keep sifting through it in order to get on to the next task. Most desks and offices are miniature extensions of the occupant's home, over-flowing with mugs, calendars, clocks, radios, stuffed animals, knickknacks, plaques, awards, exercise equipment, stickers, posters, photos, charts, signs, clothing, shoes, magazines, posters, photos, charts, signs, clothing, shoes, magazines, books, catalogs, paperweights, and every kind of organizer imaginable. There's also office equipment and its instruction manuals. With all of that in the way, how can anything get done?

The biggest problem with office clutter is that it reflects badly on you as a worker and it interferes with a job getting done well. Things are inevitably lost in the midst of office clutter, and sometimes those things are critical. All it takes is one lost airline ticket or misplaced document to prove how much harm clutter can do. How many times have you had to search through piles in order to find things you need? How many things have you lost only to find months later?

Clutter slows you down and it creates confusion. It's expensive because your company pays for every minute you spend searching for things you've already done.

If you work in an office, you have a responsibility to keep it looking professional. The problem is that clutter gathers gradually—one photograph turns into several, and eventually there are half a dozen shots of family and friends taped to the file cabinet. But the more you make your office "comfortable," incorporating outside hobbies and favorite things, the more distracted you will be from your work.

Also, we don't see our own clutter as clearly as others do. If you think the appearance of your office doesn't matter because at least it's cleaner than Joe's down the hall, think again. Your boss won't be impressed because she knows that part of doing efficient work is having an efficient work space.

DESK CLUTTER

Some people mistakenly think that a cluttered desk looks like a productive desk, but keep in mind, the people who have the cleanest desks are the ones at the top of the chain of command. Just as you dress for success, have your office and desk dress for success.

When your desk looks like a train wreck, you are sending a message that you have lost control. But a neat appearance can go a long way toward making your work look good.

Keep you work surface clear. The only things you should store on top of your desk are the things you use every day: computer, Rolodex, and pen holder. Office supplies like your stapler, tape dispenser, and paper clips can be coordinated and displayed if they are used every day. If not, keep them out of sight. Always have a trash can within reach of your desk. Think of this trash can as another storage space, reserved for useless or obsolete items.

Also consider how you use your desk drawers. Pens, paper clips, stapler, and tape can be dumped into a top drawer where they'll still be convenient but out of sight so they won't distract you or interfere with your work space.

Go through your desk drawers starting with the bottom ones. You'll be amazed at what you find—things you don't even remember putting there; things you'll never need for anything. Throw it all out. Free up that space for things you use infrequently.

Knickknacks

Knickknacks, mementos, and souvenirs are the most notorious desk clutterers. If you must personalize your space, do so in a restrained way. If your coworker gives you a tiny brass lion or china figurine for your desk, keep it there for a month or two. Then take it home and throw it away. Knickknacks are supposed to be transitory, and in the workplace it is essential that junk doesn't collect. The same thing goes for the macaroni sculpture your child made for you—it doesn't belong in your workplace.

Souvenirs from your career are a special category. One or two can remind you of the most exciting or best aspects of your job, or how far you've come along. But these unique things are quite different from the normal souvenirs you may pick up while doing business: hats, signs, samples, bits of machinery, mugs, and so on. Throw these away.

A photograph or two on your desk makes for a nice decoration. But four or five photographs are clutter. Frame photographs rather than taping them to the wall over your desk. Presentation counts more than you realize when it comes to your work environment, and the care you put into the little things will be noted.

The one type of desk decoration that should be avoided at all costs are little signs: "Working Hard or Hardly Working," "I'd Rather be Fishing," or "World's Best Mom." These are not work-related and they trivialize you before you open your mouth. And putting signs with sexual innuendo can be office suicide.

Clear off your desk after you're done working. Or clear it off every week. It depends on the types of projects you do. Regularly go through everything and make it your objective to get rid of anything you don't use. When you come to work fresh in the morning, you won't spend time sorting through yesterday's work. That's a sure opening for procrastination.

After you've cleared the clutter from your desk, you will be able to determine if your work space is large enough for your needs. Sometimes, even when the clutter is eliminated, the problem is that the area is too small.

COMPUTER CLUTTER

Computers bring with them their own clutter issues. Special accessories—hardware, software, floppies, interfaces, manuals, cables, CD-ROMs, modem—as well as the information clutter of backed-up versions, printed out copies, copies saved to disk, and the ever-cluttered hard drive mean taking action to prevent your computer from taking over your home or office. Computer files need to be kept as up-to-date as paper files, otherwise your computer will be cluttered.

Hardware and Software

Your hard disk and operating systems are the heart of your computer. If you keep packing your disk drive with programs, eventually you won't have room for documents and the overall performance of your computer will be affected. If you are running low on disk space, you will need to uninstall some of the software that you never use. Check your manual to find out how this is done in your particular system.

CD-ROM

A CD-ROM drive plays multimedia CDs with text, pictures, video clips, and audio clips. The best space-saving computer device is having an entire encyclopedia on one CD-ROM. What formerly took up two shelves to hold the thirty-book set of Encyclopedia Britannica now takes up less room than a paperback book.

Backups

If you've ever had a hard drive fail, you've learned the terrible lesson of what happens when you don't back everything up on floppy. You also risk losing it to a virus or electronic failure when you don't back up your work. Get in the habit of backing up your files daily; you won't have to think about it after a while. It will be automatic.

Of course, back-up disks mean clutter because duplicates are inherently clutter. You only need to save back-ups as long as the project is viable. Correspondence, notes, and prior versions don't need to be saved, and most disks can be tossed once the project is done. Afterward, you only need one copy, which can be transferred onto a fresh disk that holds completed projects for the year. Consider keeping your copy on disk rather than a hard copy because it frees up space on your hard drive.

CLEANING YOUR COMPUTER

Computers attract dust and lint faster than anything else in the home or office. They've got little fans inside that suck in the bad air, and the static electricity acts like a dust magnet. This stuff can deposit on the sensitive electrical components, clogging your computer vents, and heating up the works. Make sure you clean your computer with a feather duster or paper cloth and cleaner at least once a week.

The same goes for the keyboard, though it can be harder to clean. Turn off the computer so the keystrokes won't stall the computer. Turn the keyboard upside down or pop off the keys to get at stuff that's stuck underneath.

There are vacuums made for computers that you can buy if you live in a particularly dusty or dirty area. You can also get a can of compressed air like photographers use to clean negatives. It blows a steady, focused stream of air.

Vacuum all the vents and holes from the outside of your computer, including the floppy drive and CD-ROM drawer. If you have the brush attachment for your vacuum, put it on the computer vacuum while you're doing this.

Never use a Dust Buster or regular vacuum cleaner on the inside of your computer. These vacuums can suck components off your circuit boards and emit enough static electricity to fry your computer.

ELIMINATING CLUTTER

If your desk is nearly buried, you're going to have to do some major decluttering. Come in early or stay late to take care of it. You don't want to gather an audience during the effort. You also don't want to irritate your boss: Your company already paid for the time it took you to get your office in such terrible condition, it won't want to pay to fix it. Besides, getting rid of built-up clutter can be an appalling sight.

One of the best ways to clear off desk clutter is to take everything off your desk and clean the surface. This means everything. Every piece of equipment and every cup of pens that's gathered. Then only put back the things you use. The rest is clutter.

Drawer clutter is more insidious. Be ruthless and throw away every object you pick up that doesn't have an immediate and clear use.

Beware of too many organizers. One plastic device to hold paper clips and sort pens is an organizer; two or three are clutter. Keep only one cup or container on your desk to hold pens and pencils, not two or three. Keep a few boxes of supplies neatly in a drawer. Then if you run out of pencils or pens, you can effortlessly replenish your supply.

Clutterers collect little bins, racks, stacking trays, and slotted containers in order to stash more stuff. These masquerade as organizers, but they're really clutter holders. You don't use that stuff, so why keep it around?

Unless you have an immediate and frequent use for packing materials, they are clutter: cardboard boxes, Bubble Wrap, old ribbons, plastic bags, cardboard pieces, tubes, cartons, Styrofoam, and so on. When you do have to send something, you'll probably want to use packing material that looks fresh anyway.

Anything that is yellowed, hardened, expired, cracked, rusted, crumbled, or torn should be thrown away immediately. Dried-up felt-tip pens, used-up highlighters, leaky ballpoints, and eraserless pencils should also be thrown away. And get rid of all those orphaned pen caps.

Old or broken office equipment including drawer

knobs, armrests, casters, or miscellaneous screws or bolts should also be disposed of. And get rid of those old cartons, cases, and packing crates. Even if it was the original box a piece of equipment came in, you won't need it again. If you move to a new office, pack it in a new box. If it breaks, carry it to the store without a box.

Throw away duplicates of supplies. Why keep six bottles of Wite-out? Even though getting rid of duplicates is one of the easiest ways to rid yourself of clutter, many find it hard to part with their extras. Most people will tell you that they keep duplicates because they might need the extra one someday. But you don't need two of most supplies such as staplers, staple removers, erasers, rulers, and letter openers. You can only use one at a time, so get rid of all but one.

Say good-bye to furniture duplicates, too. Do you really need an extra chair for stacks of papers and folders? If people can't sit on your extra chair because it's piled with junk, perhaps you should get a file cabinet instead. At least that piece of furniture will serve its intended purpose.

CLUTTER TRAPS

Offices have their own unique clutter traps. Be aware of these to ensure you don't get lulled into a cluttered existence.

Freebies are a clutter trap. When you go to a seminar or convention, you get swamped with freebies. Follow this guideline: anytime something is free, it's clutter, whether it's a poster, brochure, sample, button, or tote bag. Things that come free in the mail or along with your order of office supplies are also clutter. Calendars, memo pads, magnets, and stuff with other people's logos on it are all clutter if you don't have an immediate use for them.

Get rid of parts and components that don't have a clear and immediate use. These clutter traps come with office equipment and often stick around longer than the original piece. Supply drawers aren't meant to hold plastic covers, electrical connectors, attachments, wires, and accessories that have no defined purpose.

Old reference material like phone books, catalogs, directories, manuals, and price lists should be thrown away as soon as the new one comes in. Out of date material is always clutter. You might be surprised to know that desk sets are clutter traps. Most people don't need the entire set, and they take up a lot of room in your work space.

You shouldn't crowd every plaque and award you've gotten onto your walls. If an award helps your professional prestige, then proudly display it. If it is an intra-office commendation, then file it in a folder with your resumé.

People also get gifts from clients or solicitors. Don't feel compelled to save these things for fear of offending anyone. You could always pare your office down to clean efficiency, and say your boss requested that you keep it that way. Set a good example when you give gifts—give something that's consumable like cookies or fruit, or give something transitory like flowers or balloons.

Never make your office too much like home. You don't need a coffee machine of your own, slippers under the desk, and a selection of nail polish in the drawer. Your office is for working, and you should focus your environment to help focus your attention.

Helpful Hints

- Clutter takes up valuable time you should be spending on getting your real work done.
- Clear off your desk after you're done working.
- Avoid collecting little bins, racks, stacking trays, and slotted containers in order to stash more stuff.
- There are many system optimization utilities available that can help you unclutter your computer and improve its operation.
- Don't clean the inside of your computer unless you know what you're doing.
- Getting rid of duplicates is one of the easiest ways to get rid of clutter.
- Freebies are a clutter trap.
- Another clutter trap is making your office too much like home.
- Set a good example when you give gifts—give something that's consumable like candy or cookies, or transitory like flowers.

10 : *Clutter Sweeps*

There are certain times that you'll need to do a full-scale clutter sweep. Some people use the psychology of spring to prompt them to clean their home, clearing out the old and freshening the house. Others take advantage of a holiday weekend to tackle the built-up clutter. Some let their clutter gather until they are forced to deal with it. This chapter is dedicated to some of the best times to do a full-scale clutter sweep.

MOVING

Moving is the best time for getting rid of existing clutter from your life and organizing new systems to keep clutter from accumulating in our new home. Make decisions as you pack as to whether you use certain objects or not. Keep an open box in every room to collect the junk you don't use. The boxes can be thrown out when you're done packing.

Throw away all those mementos that have been packed away and neglected. And get rid of everything you aren't interested in displaying in your new home. Save the things you aren't sure of and put them in a box together. If there's no place for them to go in your new home, throw the box away.

As you're packing, examine the floor plan for your new home, paying particular attention to the storage areas. You can decide the basic layout of your home while packing up what you own.

Sorting

Just as you store similar objects together, pack your household categorically. Sort as you pack, leaving several boxes open to gather similar objects. Duplicates and unused objects will then be easier to detect. Throw them out to make unpacking and storing things in your new home easier.

Pack boxes according to the room the objects should be in and clearly label the box on several sides with the room and a brief checklist of what the box contains. Always keep likes together—try not to mix towels with your blow-dryer, or videos with photographs, even if these will be stored in the same room.

People tend to think the goal of packing is to fill up a box as fast as you can. Packing boxes with a lot of different objects that should be stored in different places will only create a nightmare when you're unpacking. You'll have half-empty boxes everywhere and you'll tuck things into the first convenient space just to get them out of the way.

As you pack your books, CDs, cassettes, and videos, sort them according to the guidelines in chapter 8 and organize them by category. When you reach your new home, it will be easier to unpack and shelve them.

It can be traumatic for a child to learn how to get rid of clutter, while he or she is being forced to give up friends and a familiar environment. Don's make your children get rid of any of their possessions unless it is absolutely necessary. If they see you disposing of a large amount of clutter, they may want to join in. Make sure they only throw away things they don't play with. Sometimes children mistakenly offer up a stuffed animal or doll that is a constant playmate. Gently dissuade children and ask them to help you decide which household items should go instead.

GARAGE SALES

If you've allowed clutter to build up for years, it's probably a good time to host a garage sale. That way you can clear out your attic, garage, and storage spaces all at the same time and feel like you're getting something in return. You'll also have the pleasure of knowing that other people want your precious objects—they'll even pay you money to carry them off. For confirmed clutter collectors, this can be a very satisfying experience.

Don't worry about putting true *junk* out for sale. That's often the first thing that goes. When you see a broken fan, another person sees replacement blades for his or her fan. When you see a broken lamp, another person sees an easy rewiring job.

Anything can be sold at a garage sale: clothes, dishes, sports equipment, books, appliances, furniture, knickknacks, videos, or what have you. The more variety and number of objects you have for sale, the better.

Don't save up for a garage sale. If you have your clutter somewhat under control, don't save boxes of stuff for that mythical garage sale in the future. Garage sales work best with households that are going through a huge sweep.

If you need motivation, get together with a couple of neighboring families and hold a garage sale for your block. This will attract more people and generate more sales. And you'll have the added psychological boost of having agreed to do a sale, so you'll have to go through with it.

I've seen garage sales where everything is tagged and displayed attractively, but I've also seen ones where everything is still in boxes and you have to rummage through old bicycle parts, Tupperware, and extension cords all piled up on one another. Tables for displays and racks for clothing are fine, but you can also use boxes and place things right on your driveway. People come for the bargains, not the atmosphere.

Signs are the best way to get people to come to your sale. Post a sign at the nearest large intersections. Keep it simple: GARAGE SALE, 3 HOMES AT BROWN & OAK. Then post arrows with "Garage Sale" leading to your house. If you look around your town for similar signs, you'll find out whether Saturday or Sunday is the best day for a sale.

Go to a couple of sales to find out what people charge for things. You might be surprised. You can also go to thrift stores to see what they charge for used objects. Whether you tag the items or just decide on the spur of the moment, price in round number—five dollars or fifty cents.

Don't sell antiques. Leave that task to the professionals who can give you the right price.

As for the stuff left behind, don't pack it up and save it. Put it in big garbage bags when you're done and throw it away—or give away everything left to a thrift store or charity at the end of the day.

MILESTONES

Milestones in your life are the perfect time to clear away clutter. You're probably looking ahead to the future, and it will be easier to let go of the past when you know new things and experiences are coming your way.

If you're getting married or your significant other is moving in, you owe it to him or her to do a clutter sweep to prepare for the arrival of his or her things. The same is true when a new baby is on the way. Another good time is when you retire or change careers, or when your children move out of the home.

It's very important to make room for new arrivals. Psychologically as well as physically, you have to prepare. Take a real look at your life and see where your things fit into the future. Do you have to keep all those reminders of the past when you're on the cusp of positive changes? And how will the new arrival feel if there's no space for him to make your shared residence feel like home?

When children leave, take a look at what you have around the house. You'll probably be storing a few boxes for them for years to come, but do you have to keep their rooms exactly the way they left them? Turn your child's old room into a guest bedroom or a den—or perhaps a home office or workroom. You can always put a sofa bed along one wall for visitors.

When you retire, you may be surprised how much better you feel about the future when you clear out the past. Get rid of everything you no longer use and free up space for new activities and interests. You may even want to move, and clearing away clutter first will make the experience much easier.

Changing careers, or being between jobs, on sabbatical, or a leave of absence are good times to unclutter your home or office. It's a chance to brush off the old and reassess your life to prepare for something new. If you lost your job unexpectedly, eliminating clutter can also be a way to come to terms with the change. By taking control of your things, you'll feel better prepared to take control of your career.

Sometimes even just a break in the routine is a good time to get motivated to eliminate clutter: a snow day, vacation, rainy Saturday, or a long weekend. All you need is a couple of large plastic bags to change your life.

Helpful Hints

- Moving into a new home is the best time to remove clutter from your life and organize new systems to keep clutter from accumulating in your new space.
- Sort as you pack, leaving several boxes open to gather similar objects.

- Since moving can be traumatic for children, don't make them get rid of any of their possessions unless it is absolutely necessary.

- A garage sale will help you clear out your attic, garage, and storage areas, and make you feel like you're getting something in return.

- If you need motivation, get together with a couple of neighboring families and hold a garage sale on the same day on your block.

- Milestones in your life are great times to clear the clutter form your home.

11 : *Uncluttering Your Time*

What does clutter have to do with time? We already know that clutter takes up too much of your precious time. But did you know that your time can be cluttered too?

If your home and office are cluttered, quite likely your time is cluttered as well. If you swing between procrastination and frantic activity, then your time is cluttered. If you are always late or forgetful in what you need for your day, then you need to organize your time as well as your things. Any task that is left half done is clutter.

Organized people get a lot more done. You, too, can learn the few simple rules of time management that will allow you to prioritize and deal with your work.

Prioritizing is important if you continually have days when you feel like you're not accomplishing anything. If you aren't getting important tasks done, you'll never be satisfied. To define what is most important in your life, make a list. Spell out your goals—six months, one year, two years, five years. Do you want to advance in your career? Buy your own home? Raise children? Retire? Writing it down will help you pinpoint the priorities in your life and make your goals more real for you. That which furthers your primary goals are your most important tasks and should take priority over everything else.

TIME MANAGEMENT

Cluttered time is the inability to organize your work and get anything done. Your time is affected buy the way you approach the tasks before you and the systems you use for completing them.

Organizing your time involves making decisions, just like getting rid of clutter. You can't have hassle-free time without making a few rules for yourself. Through good time management, you'll have the right tools and habits to improve the way you perform a task.

Plan Ahead

When you begin a task, take a moment to think about what you're about to do. Do you have the resources you need? The tools? A proper work surface?

Gather the things you'll need to get the first part of the task done. Most people get sidetracked when they have to search through four drawers to find a pencil in the middle of something, or make several phone calls in order to track down information. By the time they get done, they've allowed themselves to waste time that should have been spent completing the task.

Consider how much time a task or project will take. Break a larger project down into manageable chunks and complete each task before moving on. For example, when you're writing a letter, get it done rather than leaving the letter printed out but with no envelope addressed or stamped. If you take the extra five minutes to finish, you can move on to the next task with a sense of satisfaction and completion.

Keep a clock in every room to avoid the excuse of not knowing the time. Then you can plan ahead and figure out what time you will finish each task.

Keep Records

Don't rely on memory alone. Use the resources you have to write down appointments and ideas, as well as the things you need to get done. Jotting down notes about everything will save you from making easily avoided mistakes.

Don't clutter your mind with notes even if you do have a great memory. Separate notes into lists entitled "Call," "To Do," "To Buy," and so on. This will give you a visible map of everything you have to do.

To keep your notes from becoming clutter, write everything down in one place. When you use Post-its for messages and reminders, throw them away rather than letting them accumulate. They inevitably stick to other pieces of paper and get lost anyway.

Develop a system that works for you. A daybook works for many people because it is portable. If you're setting up a system for your home and kids, use a large wall calendar. Put stars by your priorities or mark each task with the letter of the week it must be done by.

Double Your Time

Use the time you spend commuting or standing in lines to do other things. Go through your bills, read or listen to a good book, write a letter. Do mending or wash dishes while you talk on the phone, or exercise while watching television.

A little planning ahead each week can help shorten the time you spend on tasks. Combine errands—pick out a birthday card on your way to the bank, or take your shoes to be fixed while getting the paper.

Create Forms

Preprint or type labels for frequently used addresses and your own return address. This will speed up your mail processing.

Use forms for information gathering or delegating, such as self-addressed stamped postcards confirming reservations and appointments. You can also have cards made to accompany information, with boxes to check for action: "FYI," "Please Call," and space to write a note.

Create form letters for your correspondence, whether it's a letter to accompany your resumé or one that pertains to a particular project.

Read Effectively

Learn to skim rather than read every document. The first and last paragraphs, and the first and last sentences in a paragraph usually contain the most important information. In some cases, you have to get past the introduction to find the meat of the subject.

When you're faced with a large amount of material to be read and you don't want to toss the entire pile, there is an alternative. Skim through the periodicals first. Don't read them, just check to see if there's anything interesting. If there is, rip it out for later reading. After you've gone through the magazines and newspapes, you'll have a much smaller pile of clippings.

Carry a few clippings at a time to read when you're in line at the store or bank. It's likely you aren't as interested in the article as you thought, and it may only take a few moments to discard it. Throw away everything you've read before you get home.

Some people set up a specific time during the day to read—with their coffee, before bed, or before dinner. As with anything else, setting a schedule will ensure you spend more time doing things rather than procrastinating on them.

Services

There are people who will do most any unpleasant or time-consuming chore for your for a fee. Weigh the amount of time you spend doing something against how much it costs to have it done for you. There are many things you are doing now that can be done more efficiently by someone else.

Rather than arguing with your spouse or housemates about cleaning the house, hire a once-a-week cleaning person to come in. He or she will do the deep cleaning— mop floors, vacuum, clean the bathrooms and kitchen. Then your tasks are reduced to keeping the place neat and the clutter under control. The amount of money it costs to have your cleaning done could be well worth it in saved time and stress.

There are also a number of weekly or monthly chores that can be done professionally. You can pay to have your laundry done, like you do with your dry cleaning. And work can be contracted out, from repairs to paying someone to mow the lawn or sweep the walks.

Pick up and delivery services can eliminate wasteful commute time. Some stores allow you to call in and order groceries to be delivered. Laundry services offer pick-up and drop-off service. Getting take-out food delivered is the biggest time-saver of all—it only takes a phone call. Usually all its costs is a tip and sometimes a small fee.

INTERRUPTIONS

Most interruptions are caused when what you want to do conflicts with what someone else wants your to do. That creates cluttered time.

Figure on interruptions in life. It's how you deal with them that counts. Pad in extra time for interruptions by figuring that however much time you estimate a project will take you, it could take 20 percent longer because of interruptions.

Whenever you can, simply note when something occurs so you can deal with it after you're done, rather than letting it interfere with the task at hand.

Of course, some things won't wait. If you have to, deal with the matter and get right back to what you were doing—but don't use it as an excuse to do other tasks related to the interruption. Otherwise, you'll do bits and pieces of projects and jobs and never get anything accomplished.

Work

Ask friends and coworkers to give you notice before dropping by. Set certain hours that are off-limits. By always saying you're too busy right after lunch to stop and chat, people will learn to avoid you during that time, yet still leaving you accessible for social interaction at other times in the day.

If you are continually being interrupted by people who work for you, perhaps you're not fully explaining their tasks or giving them the information they need to get the job done. Keep that in mind the next time you delegate a task, and give them more information. Delegation means giving a job to someone—you shouldn't have to be watching their every move.

Consolidate appointments into a block of time rather than scattering them throughout the day, which only breaks up the time you could spend concentrating on projects.

Telephone

Your phone area should be clear of all paperwork except for message pads, providing you with a free surface for whatever you might need to do while you're on the phone. Take a note of what you need to do or information you received during the call.

If phone calls constantly interrupt your work, set aside a certain block of time when you will be free to take calls. Let your voice mail pick up calls, or, if you work from home, invest in an answering machine to screen your calls. Return all your phone calls during a specific time period rather than responding to each one separately. Turn off the sound if screening calls is too difficult for you. That can be your best time-saver if you always allow yourself to get interrupted. Of course, if you're a surgeon you must be accessible, but how many of us are involved in life-or-death situations? Almost anything can wait for a half hour.

When you leave a message for someone, specify a block of time when you will be available for a return call. That will prevent you from missing another call and having to call back again.

A cordless phone is a great time-saver. You can walk anywhere and do what you need to do without getting tangled in the cord. However, most people complain that the headset is too narrow and smooth to be held between the shoulder and jaw, so it's hard to do other things while talking on a cordless phone.

Learn how to end phone conversations effectively. For example:

- Refer to the main question or problem of the conversation. "Well, let me look into this and I'll get back to you."
- Tell the person on the other end that you need to call someone else soon or you have to go to a meeting. "I'd like to talk some more but I have to go in a minute."
- Sprinkle reminders in your sentences that the conversation will be ending soon. "All right, let's make sure we have this straight before we hang up."
- End the call yourself if it is dragging on. Etiquette says that the person who made the phone call ends it, but do it yourself if you need to. "Thanks for bringing that to my attention. I'll talk to you again soon."

Family

Whether you work in an office or from home, you have to be consistent in order to teach family members to respect your work hours or private time. Tell them when you do not want to be interrupted, and unless it's an emergency, then don't let yourself be interrupted. Tell them it will have to wait until you're done or until you get home.

If your family continually interrupts you, determine the most frequent types of requests. Try to anticipate the problems and solve them before they arise. Set up convenient snack foods for children, and tell them when you will have time to sit down with them later to help them do homework or to play.

A large monthly calendar with everyone's schedule clearly marked on it can be the biggest help in organizing family time. Mark down appointments, sports practices, parties, lessons, scout meetings, school events, and play dates. Also, mothers and fathers should mark down their major events so children feel secure in knowing what will happen—father is going away on a business trip next weekend, while mother is taking Friday afternoon off to go to the doctor.

PROCRASTINATION

People procrastinate for different reasons. Determining the reason can help you get over your inability to start something.

Evaluate each situation. Sometimes all you have to do is recognize a certain pattern in order to stop falling into it. Do you make a phone call when you are supposed to be working? Do you get up for more coffee? Forcing yourself to not give into certain delaying habits can become a new habit in itself. This sections presents tips for when you can't seem to get started on projects or finish them.

Manipulate Time

Here's a simple trick: Record the due dates of projects and the times of appointments on your calendar as slightly earlier than they really are. If you have a meeting at 1:00, mark it down as 12:45 so you get there on time with everything you need. Sometimes those extra minutes you left yourself before an appointment is when you remember things you almost forgot. It can also give you time to mentally prepare.

If a report is due on Monday, note that it's due on Friday. That way, you have padding in case something goes wrong, or if you just didn't calculate the project time accurately. Up until the last minute, try to forget that you have a few extra days or minutes. The psychological impact of seeing an earlier date will help speed you along. This may prevent you from delaying the start of your project.

A similar method is to set deadlines for yourself—the project will be one-third of the way done by Monday, and halfway completed by Friday, and so on. Tell yourself you have to write that letter by 4:00 P.M. You'll be amazed how well it works.

If you continually miss deadlines, set yourself at least one deadline a day and do everything in your power to meet it. Once you have that under control, set two per day. You'll gradually learn to speed up your work.

Render the Task Into Smaller Pieces

Break down large projects. Somehow people find it easier to face a score of little tasks than one enormous job. It won't take less time, but you will only have to deal with a fraction of the project at a time, rather than having to face the whole thing at once.

For example, if you estimate it will take you two days to scrape and repaint the garden furniture, first assign yourself the task of gathering and washing the furniture to prepare it. Once you're started, it'll be easier to keep going.

Sometimes all it takes is one movement forward to break the barrier of procrastination. Define the first small step or the easiest part of the project and begin with that. It doesn't matter if that particular task doesn't have to be completed until the end of the project. Just as directors often shoot films with the scenes out of sequence because of convenience, many unwieldy projects can also be broken down into its component parts.

Don't wait for a huge block of time to do the entire project. If you have to organize your bookshelves, do it one shelf at a time. Even if it takes weeks to complete, you'll see progress in the shelves you get to first.

Allowing yourself a series of successes during a project is a good way to keep encouraged until the end. Beating yourself up over what you haven't done yet rather than recognizing that you're halfway there interferes with your productivity. Each small success gives you a second wind for the next stage.

Stop Being a Perfectionist

Many times people set their standards too high for themselves. They need bookshelves, so they design an elaborate floor-to-ceiling structure that they will never have the time to build. Why not set your sights on a bookcase that's prefabricated? All you have to do is order it and pay for it when it arrives.

Even if your living room would ideally look better with built-in bookshelves, be practical. The reason you're getting bookshelves is because you need them—so get them now.

Don't wait until you have the money or the time to "do it right."

Don't aim to get a job done perfectly: Aim to get it done well. I've met people who frighten themselves out of doing all kinds of things because they know they can't do it perfectly. Get the job done as best you can, and next time you'll do it better. Think of it as a learning experience rather than an end product.

If you worry that you're not going to do it right, take that first step anyway. Just because some writers throw away the first draft and even the second draft of their books doesn't mean their stories are bad. You have to go through the preliminary steps to reach the end result.

Sometimes you have to accept your own failings rather than trying to be perfect. If you can't do anything but procrastinate, give in to the inevitable. But instead of filling up your time doing little things, don't do *anything* for ten minutes. Don't read, don't talk to anyone, don't take phone calls. After a few minutes of simply thinking about the project waiting for you, undoubtedly you'll get an idea of something you can do right now. So do it.

Unpleasant Tasks

The most typical reason for procrastination is that the task is not very interesting, or it's even downright unpleasant. Why start mowing the lawn or cleaning the toilet when you could just sit there and daydream?

We learn in childhood that basically if we ignore something, somebody else will come along and do it. Even if we eventually have to do it, we've managed to put it off for a while. But that's worse than simply diving in and taking care of the task.

For unpleasant tasks, reward yourself when you're done. If you do two more sales calls, you can go have a cup of coffee. If you clean off two more shelves, you can quit for the night. The satisfaction of getting a job done plus the "reward" will set up a positive pattern in getting things done.

Rewards can be little things like taking a fifteen-minute break, reading an article, watching a TV program, or going out for a walk. The carrot of reward almost always works better than the stick of punishment. If you chastise yourself into doing things, you'll have both the unpleasant task and the unpleasant feelings that prodded you into doing it. Is there one type of task you regularly procrastinate about? If you can, delegate it to someone else and take on a task you will more readily do.

Take a look at your work environment. Make it as pleasant as possible—play some music, wear comfortable clothes, or open the window wide to let some fresh air in.

If telephone calls constantly interrupt unpleasant tasks, then set your answering machine to record calls with the sound turned down so you're not tempted to pick up. You can block out a half hour of time this way, then reward yourself with being able to return calls when you're done.

If nothing works to get you started, perhaps there are deeper reasons for your procrastination. Ask yourself why you haven't written those thank-you notes or called the travel agent yet? Why haven't you taken the clothes to the thrift store or watered the plants? What sort of resentment or ambivalence are you avoiding by not doing these tasks?

Coming to terms with the tension that surrounds your things is the best way to eliminate cluttered time. Dealing with your feelings up front and creating new habits will cut down on wasted time and allow you to get through the day more easily.

Helpful Hints

- There are a number of weekly or monthly chores that can be done professionally.
- Use an answering machine to screen your calls.
- You'll have to be consistent in order to teach family members to respect your work hours or private time.
- Record the due dates of projects and appointments on your calendar as slightly earlier than they really are.
- Set deadlines for yourself.
- Break down large projects: define the first small step or the easiest part of the project and begin with that.
- Many times people set their standards too high, keeping themselves from getting started on a project.
- For unpleasant tasks, reward yourself when you're done.
- Coming to terms with the tension that surrounds your tasks is the best way to eliminate cluttered time.

Index

Accessories, 84–85
Appliances, 43, 44–45
Articles/clippings, 21–25,
    100, 133
Attic, organizing, 72–73

Basement, organizing,
    72–73
Bathroom, organizing,
    47–51
Bedroom, organizing,
    41–42
Belts, 85
Books, 89–93

Cabinets, organizing,
    45–46
Candles, 29
Cassettes, 89, 93–95
CDs, 89, 93–95
Children
    and art projects, 63
    and cleaning, 62–63

and discarding posses-
    sions, 63–64
and moving, 124
toys, organizing, 40–41,
    60–62
Cleaning habits, 56, 59–60
    and children, 62–63
    and cleaning services,
        134
    and teenagers, 64–65
Closets, organizing, 69–72,
    75–76, 83–84
Clothing
    discarding, 79–80,
        81–83
    purchasing, 86–87
    sorting, 80–83
    storing, 82, 83–84
Clutter, eliminating
    basic guidelines, 3–5,
        19–20, 36–38
    and essential posses-
        sions, 8

Clutter, eliminating (*cont'd*)
  and family members,
    55–65
  and fear of loss, 17–19
  reasons for, 5–7
  steps for, 9–12, 16–17
Clutter sweeps
  and garage sales,
    124–26
  and moving, 122–24
  periodic, 126–27
  weekly, 4
Clutter traps, 12–16
  and documents, 98–99
  mental habits, 4–5, 7–8
  and the office, 119–21
Coins, loose, 29
Collections, of objects,
  21–22
Computer items, 115–17
Cookware, 43

Desk, 112–13, 118
Dishes, 43
Documents
  and clutter traps, 98–99
  discarding, 102
  distributing, 103
  filing, 103–8

  organizing, 97–98,
    99–102
  storing, 108–9

Family members
  children, 40–41, 60–64,
    124
  and eliminating clutter,
    55–65
  teenagers, 64–65
  and time management,
    137–38
Feng shui, 38
First-aid items, 49
Foyer, organizing, 38–39
Furniture, organizing, 37

Garage, organizing, 72–73
Garage sales, 124–26
Gifts, 13–14
Glassware, 44
Goal-setting, 129–30

Hooks, using, 77

Jewelry, 84–85
Junk, collecting, 27–28

Keys, 29–30

Kitchen, organizing, 42–47
Knickknacks, 21, 25–27,
    113–15

Linen, storing, 42
Living room, organizing,
    39–41
Loss, fear of, 17–19

Magazines, 21–25, 100,
    133
Mail, organizing, 109–10
Make-up, 49
Medicine cabinet, organiz-
    ing, 49–50
Mementos, 14–16
Miscellaneous objects,
    28–30
Moving, guidelines for,
    122–24
Music collections, 89,
    93–95

Nature, objects from, 15
Newspapers, 21–25, 100,
    133

Office, organizing, 111–12
    and clutter traps, 119–21

computer items, 115–17
desk, 112–13, 118
eliminating clutter,
    117–19
knickknacks, 113–15

Perfectionism, 140–41
Pet supplies, 65–66
Photographs
    displaying, 34–35
    organizing, 30–33
    storing, 33–34
Plants, arranging, 76
Possessions, organizing, 11,
    16
    essential, 8
    new, incorporating,
        77–78
Procrastination, handling,
    138–43

Refrigerator, organizing,
    46–47

Scarves, 85
Shelves
    building, 75–76
    organizing, 74–75
Shoes, 85–86

Storage areas
   creating, 74–75
   organizing, 67–69

Teenagers, and clutter,
   64–65
Telephone calls, 136–37
Time management,
   129–30
   combining activities,
   132
   documenting tasks,
   131–32
   and family members,
   137–38
   and form letters, 132
   goal-setting, 129–30
   hiring outside services,
   133–34

interruptions, handling,
   134–35
planning, 130–31
procrastination, han-
   dling, 138–43
skimming articles, 133
and telephone calls,
   136–37
and work, 135
Tools, 52–53
Toys, 40–41, 60–62

Videos, 89, 95–96

Workroom, organizing,
   52–53